Versatile

'Love and food are equally vital to our sanity and survival.'

Kuo Tzu (*The Tao of Love*)

Versatile

COOKING & LIVING ITALIAN

GRAZIA GIULIANI

ACC EDITIONS

ISBN 978-1-85149-683-9

British Library Cataloguing-in-Publication Data

A catalogue record for this book is available
from the British Library

Printed and bound in Italy for ACC Editions, an imprint of the
Antique Collectors' Club Ltd

Published in England by ACC Editions, an imprint of the
Antique Collectors' Club Ltd

Sandy Lane, Old Martlesham, Woodbridge
Suffolk IP12 4SD, UK

Tel. 01394 389950 Fax 01394 389999
Email info@antique-acc.com
www.antiquecollectorsclub.com

ACC Distribution
6 West, 18th Street, Suite 4B
New York, NY 10011, USA

Tel 212 645 1111 Fax 212 989 3205
Email sales@antiquecc.com

Photographers' credits

Page vi: Adam Draper

Pages 4–5, 104, 121, 122, 144, 158, 163, 164, 236 (top),
248, 250 (top), 263 (bottom left): Alessandro Feira Chios

Pages 17, 21 (top), 109: Denni Fiorenza

Pages 8–9, 39, 40, 42–43, 44, 45, 46, 47, 70, 72, 79, 84,
87, 91, 94, 100, 113, 116, 119, 132, 135, 140, 151, 153,
185, 197, 198, 201, 202, 205, 206, 207, 208, 211, 214,
217, 226, 229, 232, 235, 236 (bottom), 239, 243, 253:
Simon Smith

Page 14, 21 (bottom), 41 (right), 48–49, 63, 162, 171
(top), 250 (bottom): Grazia Giuliani

Pages 16, 25, 34–35, 127, 175, 176, 179, 181, 183, 187,
190, 220, 225, 244–247, 255, 257, 258, 259, 261, 263
(top left, top right, bottom right), 265: Abigail Murphy

Page 41 (left), 65, 256: Valentina Giuliani

Page 58: Nicole Tocco

Page 171 (bottom): courtesy of Premiata Fabbrica di Liquori
Emilio Borsi

Page 193: Cristoforo Bertolini

Front cover: Simon Smith (food photography), Alessandro
Feira Chios, Premiata Fabbrica di Liquori Emilio Borsi
(courtesy of), Simon Smith, Denni Fiorenza

Back cover: Simon Smith (food photography), Denni
Fiorenza, Alessandro Feira Chios

Petruzzi Stampa

To my mother, who is now with the angels and was the inspiration for this book

To my husband and daughters, who have eaten through this book

To the readers who will be inspired by this book

Contents

Foreword

This cookbook is about passion – passion for life, passion for family and passion for food. Some of the media would have us believe that schools and 'fast food' are responsible for our children's eating habits, but Grazia reminds us how important, fun and easy it is to inspire the next generation with simple everyday ingredients.

Her love of entertaining family and friends is clearly deep rooted in her heritage and is evident in many of these easy to follow yet adventurous recipes, which you won't find in any restaurant. Whether for a special occasion or an impromptu lunch with some pals, there are no dishes too 'chefy' to prepare. From the classic earthy flavours of the guinea fowl with celeriac to the fresh Mediterranean flavours of the octopus salad (my daughter's favourite), there is something for everyone. Indeed, this book reminds me of my daughter's 'adventurous' appreciation of food: at four, she was eating steamed mussels and, by eight, enjoying oysters and lobster!

Grazia encapsulates the spirit of family and food and celebrates it in a way you can perhaps only fully experience through a visit to Tuscany. I look forward to our next family holiday to Lucca, but, until then, I have this book. I hope that you enjoy it, too.

Richard Coates

Preface

The enjoyment of one of the primary sources of life – food – goes hand in hand with the need in life for good company, love and laughter. This book serves up generous portions of both, compiled by way of my experience of conviviality such as this, both as a child and as a mother. Drawing from memories of a childhood lived in Milan and reminiscences of Italy's vibrant social scene from the late 1960s to the early 1980s, my story sketches the gastronomic growth of a child naturally educated to appreciate fine food and 'meal time' as family time. As the Italian girl went on to become a mother in England, this early awareness evolved into a deeper social and emotional enjoyment that will endure through life.

No matter what our nationality, all parents are concerned with what our children eat. Traditionally, in Italy, one meal is prepared for the whole family to enjoy, with no distinction made between a children's menu and one prepared for adults. This book follows the same principle, but also celebrates the 'versatility' that is at the heart of Italian cuisine, and so the recipes include variations – 'for adults and children', 'for adults and adventurous children' or 'for adults only' (for example, a recipe or version of it that contains alcohol) – ensuring that each will be appealing to children and sophisticated enough to satisfy an adult's palate. In these annotations, 'adventurous children' are those who have already acquired a 'dare to try' attitude towards food, probably inspired, at least in part, by the eating habits of older family members or friends. Learning the importance of feeding both body and soul with quality food and time spent together with family and friends around the table embraces numerous considerations, such as:

- understanding produce – seasonal variation and availability, provenance and distinctiveness

- recognizing that most ingredients are grown for flavour and not for appearance, and that it is then up to a cook's ability to transform these into dishes that are pleasing to the eye and stimulating to the senses

- relishing the enjoyment of a tasty and healthy meal shared with others

- perpetuating positive eating behaviours from childhood into adult life, and so contributing to the enjoyment of long-term health, social skills and emotional well-being

- appreciating 'conviviality', not as an abstract, unfamiliar concept, but as an everyday reality lived from childhood to adulthood.

The book's 'every day' recipes, in Chapter 5, can be enjoyed equally at lunch or dinner, at informal gatherings or for a dinner party. Chapter 6's 'special occasions' dishes are dedicated to the festivities and celebrations that we Italians commemorate. The 'adventurous recipes' in Chapter 7 are daring and surprising, offering children and adults alike the thrill of a curious or unusual flavour.

A rich variety of photographic styles and other responses to our family's culinary journey are here included, too, and historical notes (*see* Chapter 4) as well as anecdotes feature throughout to feed the mind of a well-fed body – but it is this book's legacy of recipes that most evocatively encapsulates the Italian philosophy of food as nourishment for both body and the spirit.

Acknowledgements

I owe the creation of this book to the support of my loving husband and daughters; my esteemed publisher and editor; the amazing children – my heroes! – who took part in this project; the discerning eye of the photographers; my good friends, chefs and non-chefs alike; my sister, for the dear memories and all her help; Pignano, a Tuscan haven, and its unique characters; the natural, human and spiritual beauty of Tuscany, where most of this book was written; and all the inspiring people I have met in the course of my journey through food and conviviality in Italy.

I would like to express my immense gratitude to James Smith for having believed in my ideas from the beginning, when this book was just a list of points on A4 paper. Your trust and advice gave me the confidence to complete this project. Thank you everybody at ACC and to David Preston for fulfilling my vision of the book with the imaginative design.

Many thanks to my editor Kim Yarwood. Thank you for having been so encouraging, fair and funny. I couldn't have gone through those 'dawn-written emails' without the anticipation of receiving your witty, fun-filled replies!

A big 'thank-you hug' to all of the children who so enthusiastically took part in the book. You are all so special to me and to my belief. Also, an extended thank you to the parents for having entrusted me with your children for my cooking extravaganzas!

Thank you to all the photographers who have captured the versatility of this book and my style. Many thanks to Alessandro Feira Chios for his time and generosity.

A heartfelt *grazie* to the Pignano community. Living in the 'beautiful bubble' of your eco-village for a year gave me not only inspiration, but also warmth and a daily dose of healthy laughter. Thank you for your welcome, friendship and everything I have learnt with you all.

A big 'thank you' to all my good friends – chefs, 'home-made' cooks *and* 'kitchen-phobics'! Your support and suggestions meant a lot to me... your contributions to the recipes are scattered throughout the book. I would also like to thank Fiona Edmonds for spotting 'the leaks' in the book; Tamy Zupan for her patient advice on IT and mathematics... let alone eating all those dinners; Kimberly Girard for her 'rubber gloves support' and American measures crash course; Alex Clarke for coming to the rescue by letting me use his immaculate kitchen; the Schmidlin-Ackermans family for their support and for sharing their fabulous pyrolytic ovens; Zak H. Stern for tracking down that beautiful picture by Nicole Tocco I really wanted to include in the book; Fabio Maranelli and Valentina Giuliani for helping organize the photographic material; the Bertolini family for all their help and shared memories. Many thanks to Sebastian Davey, Jean Macalpine and Kenneth Draper R.A. for their professional advice and affectionate support.

As a woman and a writer, I am indebted to the love, support and encouragement my husband and my two girls have given me through life and through the experience of writing this book, practically all together as a family. Adam, Nicoletta and Sofia: I couldn't have done it without you.

I had great fun, thank you all! Anyway, as you have all been so kind, I thought I'd mention, my next project is...

Notes on ingredients

Several recipes in this book call for regional Italian ingredients, such as Tipico Lodigiano, a cheese produced in Lodi, Lombardy, while others make use of unusual pasta shapes or varieties, including bucatini, cavatelli, mafalde, orecchiette, pappardelle, pastina and tortiglioni rigati. Speciality ingredients such as these can often be sourced through Italian delis or from good quality supermarkets. Furthermore, more common, locally available substitutes are suggested alongside any unusual ingredients in the recipes, too.

The preparation and production processes of many Italian foodstuffs, including several cheeses and hams featured herein, are strictly regulated according to their Protected Geographical Status classification. Protected Designation of Origin (PDO) (in Italian, *Denominazione Origine Protetta*) cheeses, which must be traditionally and entirely produced within a specified region, and thereby acquire unique qualities, include Asiago, Fontina and Taleggio.

Parmigiano-Reggiano, Gorgonzola, Grana Padano and buffalo mozzarella from Campania are all PDO cheeses, too, and are traditionally made using animal rennet, so vegetable rennet (*caglio vegetale*) equivalents should be used if you are creating a vegetarian version of one of the dishes in which these cheeses are featured. There are now several parmesan-style non-animal rennet hard cheeses, for example, available through health food stores and specialist delis.

Extra-virgin olive oil is enjoyed at its best drizzled on food at the end of the cooking process, or as a dressing for raw vegetables, cheese, meat and fish. Recent research has also shown that olive oil is ideal for frying. It has a low fat content and so can be used generously in the frying pan to form a crust on the surface of food for even cooking. Heat the olive oil gently, increasing to the required temperature without overheating, and make sure the oil is hot before frying. When making *soffritto*, if you wish to reduce the proportion of oil used, pre-mix five portions of water to one of oil before using to soften the onions.

Finally, where ingredients, cooking utensils or processes are known by other names in different countries, alternative names have been provided here too.

Notes on measures

The metric to imperial conversions featured throughout the book are approximate and represent equivalent measurements rather than exact conversions. Follow one or other set of measurements, but don't switch between the two as there may be small discrepancies between equivalent units.

Liquid ounce measures are given as US fluid ounces (fl oz) and pint measures relate to the US pint (16 fl oz), not the imperial pint (20 fl oz). Note that the fluid ounce and the ounce (weight) are not the same measurement.

Converted butter quantities are often expressed as portions of a stick as, in the USA, butter is often bought in 100 g / 4 oz sticks.

The suggested oven temperatures and cooking times are given only as guidelines and may vary from oven to oven. Ovens should be pre-heated to the temperature specified in the recipe.

Introduction:
From child to mother

The idea of this book stemmed from a collage of fond memories and a little nostalgia for a far-gone childhood brought about by having my own children. With motherhood, the heritage of appreciation, intuition and passion for food that my mother passed on to me, along with the 'food rituals' and lifestyle that accompanies them within a traditional Italian family, became more prominent.

The first page was written sitting on a sandy Mediterranean beach, smelling the sea, tasting the salt and finding myself travelling back in time – nearly 40 years – to the coastline of Puglia in a small seaside town called Bisceglie. This was my first seaside holiday. I was nearly seven and had never seen the sea before as my family always spent the summer and almost every winter weekend in the mountains north of Milan. It was 1971 and, in those days, Italians – as a nation – went on holiday within Italy; travelling south from Milan, where I come from, or going to Sardinia, Sicily or any of the small islands was either almost exotic or reserved for people who originally came from these regions. Few Italians travelled abroad.

Italians were – and some still are – quite conservative in their tastes and will favour a single destination to which they have been going on holiday for years, having perhaps bought themselves a chalet or a coastal residence, cultivated a circle of 'holiday friends' and established that familiarity which gives us Italians comfort. They have begun venturing over the Alps and beyond the Mediterranean, mingling with the locals and trying other cuisines – but, inevitably, they will always seek out a restaurant that makes a good plate of pasta 'like mamma makes'. The journalist Beppe Severgnini once observed that, according to a British survey, 90 out of 100 Italians prefer Italian cooking to other cuisines.[1] This may sound all too patriotic, but Italian cuisine is thought to be favoured by 42 per cent of non-Italians, too!

One may be wondering why. Maybe it is because, after nearly 40 years, sitting there on that beach, the smell of the sea reminded me of early morning breakfast by the Bisceglie coast, near the port where fishermen served warm *focaccia al pomodoro* with just-caught mussels, urchins, razor shells and clams drizzled with lemon juice. Soft warm *focaccia* and seafood may sound a bit different from, say, breakfast cereal and will certainly not be everybody's cup of tea, but those strong flavours and memories have stayed with me all my life. (In all honesty, the *focaccia* was my favourite and I only later acquired a taste for mussels and clams!) This story may provoke a variety of reactions among readers: gastronomists may praise it, foodies may appreciate it and others may wonder about a child eating things that would challenge some adult palates. Responding to the latter, perhaps it is simply the innate curiosity we Italians seem to have concerning food, or maybe that parents take it for granted that a child will eat what they, as adults, eat.

In Italy, one cooks a family meal and everyone in the family eats that meal. Variations to the original recipe may be added or taken away – cheese, pepper, spices, herbs are optional – but the basic ingredients and the way of preparing the meal are the same for everyone, young and old. Conversely, in England, where I have been living for nearly three decades, there seems to be, at times, more of a differentiation between children's and adults' menus. The latter can be a feast of extremely varied and exceptionally well-prepared food, while children's menus tend to offer a much-reduced variety and simpler presentation.

Growing up with homemade jams, preserves, pickles, fresh pasta and cakes, as well as shopping at local markets and handling fruit and vegetables, learning about which to choose, looking at their colour, feeling their consistency, smelling their scent and, last but not least, exchanging glances with a dead fish's eye to determine how long the fish has been laying in the ice of the fish stall are all part of a 'knowledge'

1 Severgnini, B. (2007) *La Bella Figura: A Field Guide to the Italian Mind*. Hodder & Stoughton. [*Testa degli Italiani*, English] Trans. G. Watson. p. 26.

I have gradually picked up by doing these things with my mother, particularly during our holidays. It was family time that would develop into enjoying cooking together and culminated with a meal eaten together. I am by no means advocating that shopping with Mater should become a national pastime, but, instead, simply suggesting that creating awareness in children about what they put in their mouths could be the start of a more adventurous and, in the future, educated palate. On the same holiday, I remember waking up in the morning before my parents, feeling hungry. The easiest, tastiest breakfast was, I knew, awaiting me outside the house we rented, where an orchard of peach and fig trees lay before my eyes like the Garden of Eden. Tempted, I would pick a huge, yellow, soft, juicy peach, wash it with the hosepipe and eat it under the tree feeling very pleased with myself.

In the hot and quiet afternoons, during the so-called *ora del riposino* or *pennichella* (afternoon nap), most of Puglia came to a standstill. After lunch, almost everyone went to sleep – everyone except my mother, my sister and I, who, coming from Milan, were not accustomed to this civilized, siesta-like approach. Being in the dry southern countryside, however, gave my mother a chance to go picking *lumachine*, small snails that lived among dry sticks and sun-burnt grass. She would later prepare *soffritto*, using very finely chopped onions and garlic, olive oil, fresh chopped tomatoes and herbs – and then throw the pre-boiled snails in to simmer and flavour. It smelled delicious! My parents and sister would feast on this delicacy while I stared at them, feeling very sorry for the little tiny snails I had been playing with earlier on! My mother was unique even amongst other Italian mothers with her curiosity, experimentation and adventurous passion for food. She also overcame regional boundaries, something that in Italian cuisine is very strong; Italian food cannot truly be classified as 'national' but 'regional' as each of the 20 *regioni* can have its own version of the same dish.

Like everybody else in Milan, our family lived in an apartment. Ours had two terraces where potatoes, tomatoes, strawberries and herbs would thrive. The kitchen terrace became the headquarters for preparing the winter provision for *salsa* (tomato passata), *marmellata* (jam) and *sottolio* (pickles). These were easy to make and so much fun. Filling

recycled beer bottles with the cooked tomatoes, sneaking a spoonful of sugar into my mouth, licking the jam off my fingers whilst cleaning up the pan – these were all simple joys I cherished as a child. For me this was as natural as sharing our apartment with a variety of pets – in turn, a monkey, a parrot, a tortoise, two squirrels, a Great Dane and and hundreds of colourful fish – and the dog eating home-cooked rice and minced (ground) meat! Thinking back, now that I am a mother of two with a cat and a pond with a few fish, perhaps that wasn't quite so commonplace...!

As erratic as these recollections may sound, everything ran smoothly and easily. My mother made cooking, too, appear effortless, and, indeed, Italian food can be relatively straightforward to prepare. A basic three-ingredient recipe, *Spaghetti aglio, olio e peperoncino* (spaghetti with garlic, oil and dry chilli pepper flakes), is the epitome of this, and is a fun and versatile dish that can also be a last-minute saviour. 'Fun' because it can celebrate the end of an evening out with friends: in England, people often enjoy a 'night cap'; in Italy, they have *la spaghettata*. It is midnight or thereabouts, the night out is nearly coming to an end; a group of friends convene at someone's home, where the host proposes to boil some spaghetti, throw in the pan a generous amount of extra virgin olive oil, garlic and dry chilli pepper flakes, and gently fry for a few minutes, carefully avoiding burning the garlic. He – generally, this is an Italian male's speciality, a bit like barbequing is thought to be for the Aussies – would stir this sauce into the pasta and enjoy the *Spaghetti aglio, olio e peperoncino* with a fine bottle of red.

A variation on this 'versatile' recipe more suitable for *bambini* would be to boil and drain the spaghetti, drizzle on some extra virgin olive oil and sprinkle with a generous amount of freshly grated parmesan cheese (or similar hard cheese suitable for vegetarians). This version can be enjoyed with a freshly squeezed orange juice or homemade lemonade.

For the odd times when the housekeeping hasn't been quite so well attended to, nobody has gone shopping, the internet shopping delivery is due the day after and there is almost nothing in the fridge, spaghetti, olive oil and *peperoncino* (dry chilli pepper flakes) or parmesan can prove an absolute saviour for filling rumbling bellies. The spaghetti provides carbohydrates useful for energy, the olive oil provides 'good fats' and the cheese provides high-quality protein as well as calcium and other minerals.

The convivial custom of eating together is an authentic representation of Italy. Specific meal times exist, but may vary from region to region; lunch and dinner times are usually earlier in the north of the country, getting later as one travels to central and southern Italy and the islands. Mealtime is when generations of a family come together, enjoy being together, discuss issues together whilst eating and even argue over something. Parents teach and preach, children learn and debate, grandparents wisely observe and, at times, intervene, depending on how much they are enjoying their food and the small glass of wine 'almost always compatible' with the dozens of tablets the doctor may have prescribed.

Today, given society's different and increased pressures on a family's time together, mealtimes such as these may not be enjoyed twice a day, as they once would have been, but, given the opportunity, any Italian, irrespective of age, background or provenance, will gladly gather around the table at least once a day. Friends may pop in for a visit and end up staying for dinner, a spontaneous and large gathering where a banquet is guaranteed – although a gathering does not have to be big to warrant a banquet!

By way of a contemporary example, Serena and Giada, university students in their early twenties who were working as au pairs, came into our lives during a difficult time in our past, arriving from Sardinia with suitcases packed with empathy, exceptional manners, family values and a love for food. At lunchtime, they would cook for themselves, lay the table nicely and take time for each other to chat while enjoying their meal. Even I, as an Italian, was impressed. In our age of 'express', pre-packed and 'fast food', these two young women appreciated fine food, good table manners and a little break in such a natural way that any comment of appreciation from me would surely have surprised them, and their response would have probably been, 'What is so special about it?' or 'This is how it is, isn't it?'.

Serena and Giada could be described as 'slow food *convivia*', or enthusiasts of the international Slow Food movement, which began with Italian journalist Carlo Petrini's protest in 1986 against the opening of a McDonald's fast food restaurant in Rome's famous Piazza di Spagna. The movement celebrates sustainable food production and regional, traditional cuisine, as well as, more generally, a passion for preparing fresh meals enjoyed at a relaxed pace. In Turin, Italy, Slow Food brings together artisan food and wine producers, eco-gastronomists, chefs, academics and, above all, food lovers at its biannual Salone del Gusto and Terra Madre events.

The philosophy underpinning Slow Food inspired Cittaslow (Slow Cities), also founded in Italy, a movement through which the quality of life in an urban environment is improved through a conscious slowing of pace, recognizing the value and strength of local communities, protecting the environment and promoting local produce and products. This concept may seem almost alien to many children in today's burgeoning towns and bustling cities, but will remain precious to any of their parents whose own childhood tranquillity was tended in this way. This is certainly my experience. I lived the Slow Food and Cittaslow principles in the centre of Milan many years ago, thanks to the way of life my mother decided to embrace and with which she educated her family. This book is a tribute to her, to her family values and, last but not least, her eclectic and adventurous passion for cooking.

Nowadays, the feeling for and a willingness to return to nature and simplicity are spreading – even across the skyline of a city such as Turin. A project to cultivate organic allotments on building rooftops is taking place in the city, thanks to the initiative of an architect and the collaboration of flat owners living in the block.[2] These plots have become not only an oasis of healthy, homegrown food, but also a meeting point encouraging friendship and helping to combat the anonymous living that sometimes permeates big cities. This is not a pastime for retired people; it is the ambition of a community to promote a way of life and recognize the importance of feeding both body and soul.

In my childhood, too, our kitchen terrace and the many pots filled with vegetables, herbs and flowers formed a meeting point for our friends who would lunch and dine *al fresco* with our family. The potato crop was the highlight of the year, as we used to make *una gnoccata* (a meal made of *gnocchi*, or potato dumplings), which sometimes was just enough for three people but nonetheless shared among many, as if it was the best and only food on earth!

In addition to my own recipes and those handed down to me by my mother, this book also includes recipes passed on by other members of my family who share our love for food. A family recipe close to my heart is *Croquettes di Patate della Nonna*, featured on page 184. Every Wednesday it was market day in the area in Milan where my grandmother used to live. At the age of 85, armed with her shopping trolley and good strong legs, she would walk up and down the market 'hunting' for food for her family: from fruit and vegetables to fresh fish, she knew the right stalls, including that of the ever-shouting fishmonger with a wife who had blue eyes deeper than the colour of the sea and was always made up, with backcombed hair, as if, every Wednesday, she was going to a ball! It was the shopping, the chat and the meal planning for the family that kept my *nonna* very busy on that particular day, as almost the whole family would visit; certainly my mum, sister and I were regular attendees to her midweek banquets. Over those many wonderful Wednesdays, the dish I loved the most was her unmatchable croquettes.

Several friends, too, have inspired me with their recipes, and the ones taken from the menus of Ristorante Lo Sfizio and Premiata Fabbrica Borsi exemplify my own family's view on food and conviviality, adding professional expertise to a more emotional dimension. Quality, the continuity of tradition in the making of genuine and natural products, and the preservation of a broader heritage and old preoccupations are beliefs that go beyond the mere call of duty of their gastronomic profession. These views, shared by people who care about preserving the past as an integral part of our future, have driven this journey from childhood to motherhood.

2   *See* 'Nelle grandi città i cittadini coltivano sui tetti!', *L'Aromatario*, ADNKronos, Winter 2011, no 6: 28.

1

Mangiare insieme

Eating Together

I was one of those new mothers who probably made her life more difficult than necessary when weaning her babies: everything 'had to be' fresh, organic and homemade daily! This approach was, and still is, shared by many parents; there is no right or wrong, though, it is personal choice – and I made mine.

As is customary in Italy, I cooked one meal for the whole family, sometimes adding ingredients for the adults, in order to save time, physical energy and prevent food wastage. Seasonal vegetables were selected, steamed and then reduced to a 'mushy meal' for the baby while a 'diced and sliced' version was prepared for the toddler by adding extra virgin olive oil and cheese for flavour. For us adults, the seasoning was more robust and it turned a bland steamed courgette (zucchini) into a sauce for a quick yet very tasty pasta dish.

I gently fried one large onion, one or two garlic cloves, a pinch of mixed dry herbs, three fresh tomatoes, a few fresh leaves of basil, salt, pepper and a pinch of chilli powder. When the onions were soft – and, by this time, baby and toddler were fed – I would throw in the pan the steamed, diced courgette (zucchini)... and, occasionally, even the toddler's leftovers, which seem to become a primary source of food for new parents! These ingredients would simmer for five minutes and then be served with boiled, drained pasta. If some happened to be in the fridge,

I would dice fresh mozzarella and put it on top of the pasta when it was ready to be served, to add a touch of variety. Within half an hour, our entire family was fed.

When the children were very young, they would sit together at the table for their 'mealtime', and we adults would eat shortly afterwards – on a cleaner table! As a family, we started eating all together when the girls were, respectively, two and a half and one year old. Second-born children seem to catch up quickly with the rest of the family, but I was also fortunate in that, at the age of one, my second girl was one of those babies (then toddler and now little girl) who has a good appetite. Nothing went to waste!

This compensated for the fact that my first child seemed to suffer from more food intolerances and allergies than there were foodstuffs available. In the early stage of weaning, every time I tried to introduce a 'new food', it felt like playing Russian roulette. As an Italian, natural, varied and homemade meals were the only way I knew to feed my child, but this inherited philosophy had now become a medical necessity.

Interestingly, but perhaps not surprisingly, the worst reaction my daughter ever had was to what she now calls 'nasty squash' (a fruit-flavoured drink concentrate) that she drank at a playgroup – and which sent her to hospital with anaphylactic shock. Many commercially produced children's foods and drinks claim to be free from artificial colorants, flavourings and preservatives, but labels on such items can still be misleading, such as when uncertain ingredients are listed by alternative, scientific names.

As my eldest daughter gradually grew out of most of her food intolerances, though, the habit of cooking one 'versatile' meal for the whole family took an incrementally adventurous path, seeing more and more ingredients added to each recipe. Every time a new dish was introduced, I would explain what it was and ask the girls if they liked it or not, thereby gauging what might be altered or adapted. Through this process, I was instilling in my children something considered to be very 'Italian': we were talking about food while eating it, maybe discussing other foods in detail as well, pining for a particular recipe and then soaring through memories, experiences and fantasies. Wow – all this over a single main course? Yes, Italians do it all the time!

Variety is another important factor when it comes to preparing meals that can be enjoyed by everyone. For example, pasta dishes – surely the most celebrated of Italian fare – are never the same. A million different recipes offer a variety of tastes, ingredients and nutritional levels; pasta can be served with meat, fish and vegetable sauces, it can be boiled or oven baked and even eaten cold as a summer salad dish. Pasta itself can be made of many different grains, from the most traditional wheat to spelt, offering a variety of textures; vegetables and other ingredients added to the dough give an assortment of colours and distinctive flavours.

Offering variety to my children from a young age has seemingly resulted in a wider range of 'likeable' foods and a confident 'curiosity' for trying not so familiar recipes. I noticed that any suspicion regarding an unfamiliar shape, colour, texture or smell was overcome when a new dish was presented in a consciously appealing way. I don't mean that funny faces took over our plates at family meals, but, rather, that clean, imaginative presentation stimulated all of the senses and encouraged the children to try different dishes. A particular table setting, tablecloth or mats, napkins, plates, cutlery, condiments, glasses or cups, even a jug of water, can all be considered 'props' for the 'stage performance' of eating together. This may all sound slightly exaggerated and time consuming, and, of course, it is perfectly possible to eat ready-made noodles out of a plastic pot standing in front of the television and consider oneself 'fed', but a more enriched eating experience, such as is suggested here, offers not only enhanced health benefits, but also good manners and an appreciation of conviviality as a commonplace way of life.

In my experience, as well as that of many of my friends, if 'mealtime' at home is recognized by a child as a moment to spend with another person or the whole family, sitting at the table enjoying both food and company becomes natural and pleasurable. This recognition then broadens from the home through to public spaces. Certainly in Italy, restaurants are filled with family members of all ages sitting together at long tables and sharing the same dining area with a couple so enveloped by their love that they manage to enjoy a romantic dinner undistracted. As well as sharing space, adults and children share the menu, too, as

there is generally a single list of dishes from which to order. However, the choices are not daunting but exciting, as children will recognize most of the ingredients and can place their own order. I have seen children ordering seafood salad as a starter, or parents asking to substitute the hare sauce with a tomato sauce for their one year old... and I have also witnessed parents ordering pasta with hare sauce for their offspring without even questioning if it ought to be considered an acquired taste for a child, as grandma makes this seasonal dish, too, and grandson eats it!

Here following is an example of a traditional Italian restaurant menu from which dishes have been selected by children with great success. My family took two English friends aged six and nine to this restaurant, Lo Sfizio, and, while the boys could not be described as 'adventurous' when it comes to food, nevertheless, with the encouragement of their more adventurous companions and a menu featuring ingredients they recognized as their favourites, they ordered their own dishes – and thoroughly enjoyed them.

Menu

Antipasto (starter)

Antipasto Toscano / Tuscan antipasto

A platter of cured meats, *bruschetta*, olives, cheeses
and honey and pear conserve

Primo (soup, rice or pasta dish)

Pici allo Sfizio / Sienese pici

Handmade, thick, spaghetti-like pasta typical of
the city of Siena served with a pesto, cream, tomato
and sausage sauce

Secondo (main course)

Filetto di manzo / Fillet of beef

Fillet of beef cooked with rosemary and lemon

Contorno (side dish)

Insalata contadina / Peasant's salad

Lettuce, tomatoes, carrots, olives and tuna (onions, optional)
dressed with extra virgin olive oil, salt and balsamic vinegar

---

Dolce (dessert)

Tiramisù / Tiramisu

Sponge layered with a cream of mascarpone cheese and egg
yolk and decorated with cocoa powder

Lo Sfizio is an inspirational restaurant set in the hills around Siena that my family and I have visited many times. Mother cooks, father and son are at the 'front' of this family affair... The love of food, the simplicity in the preparation of ever-so fresh ingredients, the commitment to let the flavours speak for themselves and the hospitable atmosphere all combine to make this place a perfect experience of conviviality. There is no glitz or glamour in the décor, there are no Michelin stars shining above the door – but there is a generous amount of warmth in the food and in the soul of the people who make it and serve it.

The first time we visited, it was mid week, a scorching hot lunchtime in July 2010. It was late, even by Italian standards. My girls were hungry and their father was ravenous. We arrived at the village of San Rocco a Pilli (what a name!) hoping that there might be a little place there still serving food... and we found heaven.

We were welcomed by a very polite, kind and bright young man, Dani, who, having completed his university studies in cinematography, was helping his family during the restaurant's summer season before he moved out to Los Angeles. He was thrilled at the chance of speaking English with us and so chatted and chatted. His dad Pasquale then arrived at our table, very professionally took our order and disappeared once more behind the kitchen doors.

I still remember what we ordered: *Pici, Garganelli alla panna e salsiccia, Cavatelli alle vongole veraci* and *Insalata contadina*. For dessert, Tiramisu... followed by another Tiramisu (yes, it was so good that it had to be ordered twice). We were the only customers in the restaurant and Dani continued chatting, with Pasquale joining in, too, as if we were all having lunch together at their home. Then the kitchen doors swung open and Gina appeared, the creator of all those delicacies that had made us think we had reached heaven! She immediately made me feel like the long-lost daughter – and I still feel the same every time I go there! Gina's kindness, spontaneity and affection are all ingredients that infuse each delectable dish that she creates. Here, following, is her delicious recipe for *Pici allo Sfizio* for you to enjoy, too.

Pici allo Sfizio

Pici allo Sfizio

Suitable for adults and children
Preparation time: 15 minutes
Cooking time: 20 minutes
Serves 4 people

What you need
For the tomato sauce:
3 tbsp / 1½ fl oz extra virgin olive oil
2 cloves garlic, peeled and finely sliced
1 carrot, peeled and chopped into small chunks
1 celery stick, trimmed and chopped into small chunks
1 onion, peeled and finely sliced
400 g / 14 fl oz tomato passata (puréed tomatoes)
a pinch / 1/16 tsp salt

For the Pici allo Sfizio:
4 litres / 135 fl oz / 17 US cups of water
10 g / ½ tbsp / a palmful coarse sea salt
2 tbsp / 1 fl oz extra virgin olive oil
2 cloves garlic, peeled and finely chopped
2 pork sausages, skinned and crumbled
400 g / 14 fl oz tomato sauce
2 tbsp / 1 fl oz pesto
2 tbsp / 1 fl oz double (heavy) cream
400 g / 14 oz pici (or substitute with mafalde
    or pappardelle)
1 bunch flat-leaf parsley, finely chopped

Optional:
200 g / 7 oz / 2 US cups parmesan cheese, freshly grated

How you make it
For the tomato sauce:
Put the olive oil, the garlic and the vegetables in a saucepan and cook on a low heat for 5 minutes. Add the passata and a pinch / ½ a dash of salt. Simmer on a low heat for 20 minutes.

For the Pici allo Sfizio:
Bring the water to the boil in a medium-sized saucepan.

Put the olive oil in a large frying pan on a medium heat, then add the garlic and the sausage and cook for a few minutes. Turn the heat down, add the tomato sauce, prepared as above, and cook for a further few minutes.

Add the pesto and the cream, stirring the sauce for a few minutes.

When the water has reached boiling point, add salt, a few drops of extra virgin olive oil and the pici and cook for 17 to 18 minutes until al dente. If you are using a different type of pasta, simply follow the instructions on the packaging.

Drain the pasta. Mix it with the sauce in the frying pan for a few minutes.

Lay the pasta out on a serving plate and sprinkle with the chopped parsley.

Top with freshly grated parmesan if desired.

Cos'è?

'What is it?'

If a child recognizes and is able to distinguish one type of food from another, it means that they are aware of what they are eating. Presented with variety, children generally become curious about the novelty but occasionally reject an unfamiliar ingredient entirely.

In this chapter, eight children ask and answer the question 'What is it?' all by themselves. These children are my heroes: they have been happy to try almost everything I offered them, from individual ingredients to prepared dishes. Results have ranged from instant success to pleasant surprise. There has been rejection, too, of course – but in just one case! Having taken time showing the children unfamiliar fruit and vegetables, discussing them, explaining their provenance and instigating a broader conversation about the children's knowledge and experiences of trying new and unusual foods, the overriding response was that of curiosity and even excitement. I let them lead me through their exploration by answering their questions and allowing them 'convince' each other that 'that thing' was really worth trying.

Avocado by Nicoletta (9 years old)

Avocado

An avocado is dark
green almost black
and scrumptious
but it can also
be mushy if you
have squashed it
or if its gone off.
I've been eating since
I was a baby.
I like it in salad
or by itself with salt
and lemon added to
it.
The avocado has rough
that I like feeling.
It also has a big
stone in the middle
like a Mango or a
Peach.
An avocado is a
fruit because it has
a stone.
At our school in
Italy we have a
vegatable garden but
we don't grow avocado
but I would like to.

By Nicoletta

The children discovered new foods through observing and drawing them, digging produce up from the vegetable patch, helping to prepare ingredients, cooking and, finally, eating the dishes, knowing precisely what they were, with pride and relish. Presented here for your enjoyment are their accounts, illustrative and written, of the experience.

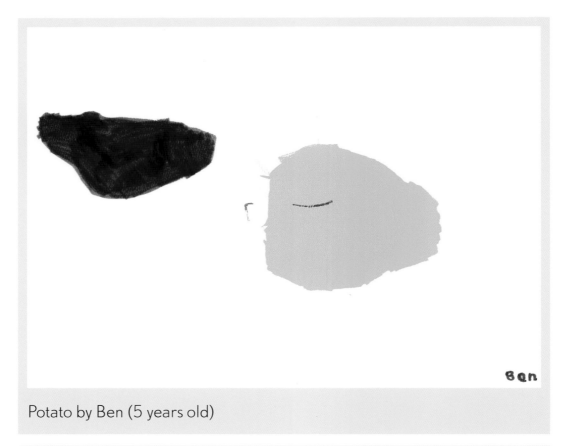

Potato by Ben (5 years old)

Tomato by Oscar (9 years old)

Potatoes

I like potatoes. My favourite way of cooking potatoes is to roast them. They are very crunchy and delicious. we grow new potatoes in our garden. it's great fun digging them up and seeing how many we get. Mummy likes to make them into a potato salad.

Ben York (age 7)

Tomatoes

I like tomatoes best when you have picked them from a tomato plant. They are warm and juicy and explode when you bite into them. My mum says I can eat them like sweets, only they are much better for your teeth. My favourite tomato is a yellow tomato because it is sweeter than the others.

Leo

Aubergine (eggplant) by Leo (9 years old)

Persimmon by Tania (12 years old)

Lemon by Hester (10 years old)

aubergine

It is purple, gree and long. At the bottom it's fat.

It looks funny.

I've seen it in shops but never tried it.

(and don't ~~want~~ wan't to try it.)

because it ~~doesn't~~ doesen't look nice

The Persimmon

The reason I chose to draw the persimmon was because
I liked its bright orange colour and because it seemed
different and I had never seen one before.
I had no idea what it tasted like or how it could be eaten,
but since it looked a bit like an unripe tomato, I expected
it to taste a bit sour.
Later, I discovered that I had been completely wrong and
that the fruit actually tastes very sweet. The persimmon's
fleshy pulp has a flavour similar to that of figs and can
be eaten raw with a teaspoon.
I would definitely want to try a persimmon in the future,
as I am very fond of figs.

Tania.

The Lemon

The Lemon is sour but also bitter.
The Lemon is also bright Yellow.
I like to make Lemonade with
my friends.

To make Lemon ade you need:

2 ½ Lemonds (Squeezed.)
5 tea Spoons of Sugar.
Fizzy water.
3 Slices of Lemon
Ice

                    Water
First get the and squeeze in the Lemon.
Then with a spoon slowly add the sugar. (mix well.)
When you have finshed add Ice and Lemon
Slices of.

by Hester

Beetroot by Sofia (7 years old)

Lemon by Angelica (8 years old)

Beetroot

Beetroot is purple.
It can be big or small.
The first time I tried it I was 3.
I really like it.

Beetroot is a vegetable.
It can be eaten row or cooked.
Beware it can Mark!

Beetroot has leaves that you can eat.
The first time I tried the leaves I was 5.
Straight from our vegetable patch.

By Sofia

I like the lemon because it tastes sour and bitter. I like sucking the lemon and chewing it because you get a better flavour. The lemon has a bright colour wich I really like. I love squrting it on my food (especially on pancks pancks). You can eat the lemon raw and you can make lots of food with it like lemon tart and cacke.

Angelica

Stagioni

Seasons and sensations

Eating involves all of our senses. The appearance of food acts as the foremost stimulus, followed by its aroma and, finally, its texture and taste are appreciated. This sequence leads to the definition of flavour as the ultimate combination of taste sensations and sensory impressions. Sweet or sour, bland or salty, bitter or sharp – all are familiar words that evoke various types of foods and our different reactions to them. A dish that features unfamiliar colours, shapes, smells or consistencies can make even an adult suspicious, let alone a child. As I have previously noted, my children's perception and consequent acceptance of food have, I believe, come about through the way in which I have presented food to them. Specifically, I quickly became aware that attractive presentation stimulated their senses – and their appetites!

After weaning, between 10 and 24 months of age, I used to prepare a *minestrina passata*, or creamy 'little soup'. A base of rice or spelt (a slightly sweet, nutty flavoured grain), chicken breast and shallots would be accompanied by various vegetables, which gave the soup a different colour and flavour for each serving. I would make orange soup, green soup, red soup, yellow soup or brown soup, depending on the use of carrots or pumpkin, green leaves or broccoli, tomatoes, potatoes or corn and lentils, respectively.

The ingredients would be mixed and reduced to a tantalizingly creamy consistency by using a hand-held food blender. The *minestrina passata* was then served in a small soup bowl atop a larger plate on which an assortment of colourful raw and steamed vegetables, along with cheese, ham and breadsticks, were presented.

To this day, throughout winter, our family enjoys *minestrina* or *brodo* (broth) as a warm, healthy start to meals. For older children, you can substitute the creamy version with one featuring small, diced vegetables and rice or *pastina* (mini pasta shapes) in a vegetable or meat stock.

During the course of writing of this book, I returned to Italy with my husband and two girls. We were based in the deep and remote Tuscan countryside, in total contrast with the lives we all knew in Milan and London, and it was in this rural idyll that I saw a younger friend of mine carrying on the old tradition of the *minestrina* for her two little boys every evening... It felt reassuring, perhaps because it brought back memories of my own childhood as well as reflecting a 'ritual' that has continued for my children. City girls or country girls, once mothers, Italians revert to traditional family customs it would seem!

While we were in Italy, my family and I travelled up and down the 'boot' and together rediscovered sights, colours, scents, aromas and tastes familiar to me from childhood. From our first encounter with the bursting Tuscan colours of summer, through to the warm earthy tones of early autumn, we witnessed the plunging of nature into the darker shades of winter and the cool light re-emerging in January and February, when the white snow, yellow sun and bright blue sky played together in a prelude to spring. We embraced each season and lived each transition, not only by being totally immersed in nature, but also by visiting shops and local markets. Our eyes, noses, hands and mouths enjoyed the yellow, scented, soft peaches, the apricots and plums, the crimson grapes, the olive picking, the crackling chestnuts and the winter greens.

The variety of the colour green of winter vegetables is extraordinary, from the deep dark green, almost black, of the Tuscan cabbage or lacinato kale (*cavolo nero*), to the lighter of the beet greens (*erbette*),

reaching the brightest green of the Savoy cabbage (*cavolo verza*). It then pales into the graduated green-to-white shades of the leek (*porro*) to stretch to the whiteness with hints of green of the fennel (*finocchio*).

The green of spinach bridges winter and spring as, although available through the year, it is at its best for freshness and tenderness from March.

The colour green becomes brighter with the arrival of the broad beans (*fave*), the first vegetable to welcome spring onto the table. It culminates with peas (*piselli*), *verde pisello* ('pea green') being perhaps the best description someone can give of a very bright green colour.

In fact, spring brings with it a range of colours, from the delicate floral tints characterizing Easter to the strongest reds of the soft fruits arriving later in the season. Market stalls are full of wooden cases (*cassette*) packed with plump strawberries and succulent cherries of many varieties. Summer erupts with the yellow and oranges of the apricots, peaches, nectarines and melons. The red, green and white of

watermelons (*angurie*, *cocomeri*), too, seem to commemorate Italian summers, the season when the fruit is best enjoyed.

The 'Anguriera', an impromptu bar where cold, sliced watermelon and soft drinks were served, was a popular spot when I was a child. In cities, by the lakes and at the seaside, 'mobile bars', comprising a small lorry, plastic tables and chairs, paper flags or any other kind of colourful paper decorations, were often set up by the side of the street. '*Andiamo a mangiare l'anguria?*' ('Shall we go for an *anguria*?') was an invitation to spend an hour with friends or family to enjoy this quenching, sweet and crunchy summer fruit chatting the evening away. Bars such as the 'Anguriera' have become a rarer sight nowadays. A few survive, though, and they will probably never entirely disappear, as they are an intrinsic part of Italian tradition and popular culture.

Italian summer colours develop into a deep rich purple, towards August's aubergines (eggplants). This firm, 'meaty' vegetable is, for me, a particularly 'visual' vegetable, not only because of its shiny purple hues, but also because its variety of shapes, from elongated and curved to round, pleases my eye every time I look at them. It is thought that the Arabs first introduced the aubergine to Spain and Sicily. For many centuries, though, gastronomists considered it an unworthy vegetable, consumed by the populace just like potatoes and mushrooms – food that was also used to feed the animals. In spite of such humble origins, though, the *melanzana* has proved very popular in modern Italian

cuisine, be it grilled, fried, oven baked, in sauces, pickled... The well-known southern Italian dish *Parmigiana* (in full, *Parmigiana di melanzane*) is made with aubergine, tomatoes, mozzarella and, depending on the region, penne pasta – all baked in the oven.

By late summer and early autumn, crimson grapes are nearly ready for *vendemmia* (harvest) and figs reign on the Italian table, utilized in both starters and desserts.

Prociutto e fichi (Parma ham and figs) is a harmonious combination in which the sweetness of the figs marries with the salty prosciutto, creating a delicious starter. Grapes, on the other hand, generally accompany cheeses at the end of a meal or are eaten as a snack. Olives, also harvested in autumn, are present in a wide variety of *antipasti* served all over Italy with a choice of regional cured meats and pickles.

Autumn sets in at different times across Italy. In the north, by mid September the air becomes chilly. In Tuscany and the central regions, mid October can still be mild. Southern Italy and Sicily, meanwhile, are often still enjoying the last days of warm sunshine.

The thunderstorms that often chase out the end of summer are a welcome sign for foragers that it is time to go to the woods in search of mushrooms. From the precious *ovoli* or Caesar's mushroom (*Amanita Caesarea*) and porcini or cep (*Boletus edulis*) to the less rare but still flavourful *chiodini* or honey mushroom (*Armillaria mellea*) or *finferli* (*Craterellus tubaeformis*), *funghi* transport the new season to the table.

The dominant colours in autumn are the deep yellows, the oranges and a variety of browns. The predominant sound is that of crackling... in the woods, leaves and twigs crackle beneath the foragers' feet as they search for *funghi* and, later in the season, chestnuts. This crackling continues in the *cucina* as the chestnuts are roasted and the aroma suffuses into the city where roasted chestnuts sellers appear at every street corner. When I lived in Milan, chestnuts were my favourite snack, and now, when I

visit my hometown in autumn or winter, I cannot resist buying a bag. In fact, I love them so much that I do not share them with any family member – they all know to buy their own!

November comes. We are heading towards winter and so back to the deep green vegetables that started our seasonal cycle – with a few notable exceptions. The artichoke (*carciofo*) – for me, the king of Italian winter vegetables – boasts a distinctive pallet of colours. Deep greens and purples on the outer leaves are peeled away to reveal tender inner leaves graduating in colour from a pale green and purple to shades of red and yellow. I find the artichoke very elegant, both in sight and taste.

My recipe for *Tortino di carciofi* in Chapter 5 presents the vegetable in an omelette-like dish. Alternatively, in a risotto, sautéed with garlic or simply boiled and dipped in a dressing of extra virgin olive oil, salt and balsamic vinegar glaze, artichoke always excels in flavour. My mother used to preserve artichokes in olive oil and later use them to

complement mixed antipasti or to provide a filling for panini all through the year.

The deep red of radicchio also breaks through the season's prevailing green in vegetables. It is known in Italy as 'the winter flower from Veneto', a northern region the capital of which is Venice. Radicchio is part of the chicory family and has two harvests: the early one in September and the late one in December. It can be enjoyed grilled, in risotto or as a salad. In Chapter 4, my recipe for *crostone al radicchio e Gorgonzola* marries the sharper taste of radicchio with creamy Gorgonzola cheese, laying them both on a slice of toasted crusty bread giving a sophisticated taste to a crostone, as an antipasto dish.

The bright orange of the *cachi* (persimmon fruits) dots the sky across cities and villages alike, as the trees, heavy with fruits, can be found in both environments. I still remember as a young child walking by a walled garden in Milan and looking up at this old tree full of *cachi*, winter after winter until my teenager years.

Vibrantly coloured oranges, mandarins and lemons abound in Sicily in winter too and make their way up to northern markets, shops and supermarkets. It is a feast of vitamin C that carries on through to early spring.

In Tuscany, my children, too, observed and recognized familiar foodstuffs, learned about new ones and tried new adventures for their palates. It was almost like going back to when they were toddlers and introducing them to a new 'realm of tastes'. When they were very young, a simultaneous presentation of four different foods contributed, I am sure, to their later appreciation of a good and healthy selection of food. Variety but also repetition of a 'not so favourite food' helped them acquire a 'dare to try' attitude towards food.

Experimenting with two slices of cheddar cheese filled with Marmite (a savoury spread made from yeast extract) to make a 'sandwich' without using bread was one of my older daughter's great culinary discoveries! I cringed… but also felt very proud of her for curiosity leads to imagination not only in cooking but also in life itself.

It would be naïve of me to imagine that my girls only like 'healthy food'. Surely almost everyone enjoys a bag of crisps or potato chips every now and then, and most people will occasionally lust after a piece of chocolate. It is therefore more about guiding children to become discerning with their snacks and recognize quality in a variety of foods. Confectionery items, for example, don't have to be artificial, coloured and synthetic. Raisins, or any other dry fruits such as mango, papaya or apricots, can easily satisfy a desire for a sweet taste. Crystallized fruit, although sugary, can still be a healthier alternative to sweets or candy. Fresh coconut is delicious and refreshing. A few homemade caramelized almonds or peanuts – if no allergy or intolerance is present – will be enjoyed just as much as the yogurt-coated alternatives sold in health food shops. You can test this theory out using my recipe, provided here!

In childhood, adolescence and adulthood, my home, both in Italy and London, has always been an open house. I have fond reminiscences of my friends gathered around my mother's table and now fresh

Caramelized Almonds

What you need
500 g / 17½ oz / 3½ US cups blanched peeled almonds
500 g / 17½ oz / 2¼ US cups caster / superfine sugar
150 ml / 5 fl oz / ¾ US cup water

How you make it
Heat a large non-stick frying pan or wok. Add the almonds. Stirring constantly, toast them. When they have lightly browned, they are ready. Make sure they do not burn.

Once lightly browned, remove the almonds from the heat and put them aside on a plate.

In a large non-stick frying pan, melt the sugar with the water. When the colour of the mixture turns amber and it liquefies (after approximately 6 to 7 minutes), stir the almonds in, constantly tossing and turning them until they are all covered with the caramel. The secret here is to patiently stir the almonds and the caramel over and over.

Lay the almonds on a cold oven tray or marble surface to dry. Store them for a couple of weeks in an air-tight glass jar away from light.

Versatility You can also use hazelnuts

Ghiaccioli di Frutta e Yogurt
Fruity Ice Lollies

These delicious frozen confections offer a healthy alternative to commercial ice cream.

How you make it
Whizz your children's favourite fruit – such as strawberries, peaches, cantaloupe melon or apricots – in a food processor. Add some organic plain yogurt and a little honey and mix well for a further few seconds. Pour the mixture into ice-lolly / 'popsicle' containers, moulds or a tray and pop into the freezer.

Lollipops

Even lollipops can be homemade and stored in air-tight
glass jars for a few weeks.

Preparation time: 5 minutes
Cooking time: 15 minutes
Makes: 10 medium size lollipops

What you need
large sheet greaseproof / waxed paper, thinly coated with butter
250 g / 8¾ oz / 1¼ US cups golden caster / superfine sugar
1 tsp butter
40 g / 2 tbsp sugar-free jam (flavour of your choice)
15 ml / ½ fl oz / 1 tbsp water
wooden sticks or toothpicks

How you make it
Cut a large sheet of greaseproof / wax paper. Spread a small quantity of
butter over the paper to avoid the sugary mixture sticking to it. In a small
saucepan, add the sugar, the butter, the jam and 1 tablespoon of water. On
a low heat, cook the mixture, constantly stirring until it becomes a smooth
paste (approximately 10 to 15 minutes).

Using a tablespoon, spoon the mixture onto the greaseproof / wax paper
forming circles. Place a wooden stick in the centre of each and cover with a
small amount of mixture to fix it in place.

Leave to set for 2 hours. Remove the lollipops from the paper and store in a
glass jar. Do not keep them in the fridge.

Versatility To clean your saucepan, fill it with water and put it back on the
heat to boil until the sugary mixture has melted. Throw the water away while
it is still hot and then wash your pan.

Chocolate-dipped Fruit

How you make it
Place a glass bowl over a saucepan half filled with boiling water. In the glass
bowl, melt some 70% cocoa solids (bittersweet) chocolate. Leave it to cool
down a little, then dip strawberries or slices of banana, apples, pears and
apricots in to coat the fruit. Chill in the fridge until the chocolate hardens
and coats the fruit, then enjoy them with your children.

memories of many of my daughters' friends gathered around our kitchen table. No matter how many of them there have been or how fussy they might be, children who have enjoyed hospitality in our home have at least tried, if not fully experienced, what for some of them was 'unusual' food, and this has always given me great pleasure. At the same time, from a young age, my girls have experimented with and now thoroughly appreciate food from a broad range of international cuisines, 'discovered' either through relishing meals at friends' homes or during family holidays. Healthy curiosity paired with an enjoyment of sharing a meal in the company of friends and family can contribute to children becoming 'adventurous' diners.

As parents, we are all concerned with the food our children eat. Using an extensive range of interesting ingredients in a diversity of dishes, each enticingly presented, should steer most towards positive long-term eating habits. It is not magic, it is not set in stone, and it is more often than not trial and error. Even if your child manages just a single mouthful, appreciate their 'brave attempt' and enjoy conviviality!

4

Note storiche

A plateful of historical notes, anecdotes and curiosities to feed the mind of a well-fed body

This chapter serves up a five-course menu of tasty, traditional Italian dishes accompanied by delicious detail on their provenance, production and preparation. Knowing how an ingredient first came to be included in a country's cuisine, or understanding what determines that a dish comes from a particular region of Italy, can add another level of gratification to any meal. Researching a selection of stories, historical references or even gourmet gossip linked to food that you later serve can offer a great source of entertainment for family and friends to share around the table.

Antipasti

Mortadella

Our menu opens with perhaps the most renowned of all Italian charcuterie, mortadella. Widely used in *antipasti* and *aperitivi*, it has been on the Italian table since Roman times. In some areas of Italy, it is known as 'Bologna', after the city in which its unique production process was first encoded in 1661, when Cardinal Farnese issued strict guidelines of quality control for this delicious meat.[1],[2] Nowadays similar rules apply through Mortadella Bologna's IGP classification, which certifies its traditional local production.[3]

It comprises delicately flavoured, cured pork sausage meat, immediately recognisable by its pink colour and the small white dots (premium fat from the neck of the pig). The soft meat is very aromatic, and some producers flavour it with pistachio nuts, but this is not part of the traditional recipe.

Mortadella can be eaten in many different ways. It can be enjoyed cut into small cubes to accompany an *aperitivo*, or sliced as an *antipasto*. Add mortadella between two slices of white crusty bread to make a tasty, traditional Italian sandwich. In this book, my recipe for chicken rolls with mortadella, *caciotta* cheese and rosemary, in Chapter 5, uses mortadella in a stuffing – this time-honoured meat is ever present.

1   Mortadella Bologna (2007) The taste of the best tradition [*Il sapore della migliore tradizione*, English] [Online] Available at www.mortadellabologna.com; accessed February 2012.
2   Regione Lombardia, Directorate-General Agriculture & Unioncamere Lombardia (2011) 'Nourishing Culture' programme and 'Food Education project', both part of the Buonalombardia initiative. [Online] Available at www.buonalombardia.it; accessed November 2011.
3   Indicazione Geografica Protetta (in English, Protected Geographical Indication (PGI)) status is part of the European Protected Geographical Status (PGS) legal framework established to protect the names of regional foods.

Primo

Risotto

Our menu of musings continues with a *primo*, which is a pasta, soup or rice dish that, in the traditional Italian chronology of courses, goes before the main course (*secondo* in Italian).

Risotto is one of my favourite *primi*, maybe because Milan is my hometown, and it was in the plains surrounding Milan, in the Po Valley, that rice became widespread towards the end of the 14th century, having been first introduced to Italy by Arab merchants in the Middle Ages. Rice quickly became part of the staple diet in northern Italy, as it was cultivated in abundance in the fertile *Pianura Padana*, where a humid climate assured bountiful harvests.

Another theory is that rice travelled from Sicily to the northern regions of Italy along with saffron. Milan was under Spanish rule for almost two centuries and one of its most celebrated dishes, *Risotto alla Milanese*, combines the rice and spices, including saffron, for which the area was known. Certainly, as the word 'saffron' is often argued to come from the Arabic word for 'yellow', a Middle Eastern influence is attributed to the dish. Jewish merchants also seem to have created a way of cooking rice with saffron, *Riso col zafran*, and to have taken this recipe to Venice.[4]

In fact, many stories surround not only the provenance, but also the origin of this regional dish, with one seeming to set a precise date for the invention of *Risotto alla Milanese*: 8 September 1574. The many versions of this account assert that in this period, amongst the aristocrats and other wealthy individuals, it was fashionable to add a pinch of gold to food at special banquets in order to bring good luck. Pharmaceutical properties, too, were attributed to gold such that diners' health was thought to benefit from its addition. Valerio di Fiandra, a Belgian glassmaker commissioned to work on the *Duomo di Milano*,

was celebrating his daughter's wedding on 8 September 1574. One of his apprentices, who had been using saffron in his colour work on the cathedral's glass, decided to add the spice to the rice served at his master's daughter's wedding in order to colour it 'gold' as the family could not afford the precious metal. There are many variations to this story, one of which sees Valerio di Fiandra as the object of a joke by his apprentices who put saffron into the rice. The mockery backfired, though, as the addition of saffron was commended by the guests who enjoyed the novelty.

The Italian gastronomist Pellegrino Artusi (1820–1911), in his famous 'cooking manual' *La scienza in cucina e l'arte di mangiar bene* (*Science in the Kitchen and the Art of Eating Well*),[5] reports two recipes for *Risotto alla Milanese*, one cooked without white wine and the other with white wine and bone marrow. The latter dates back to 1549, when the Italian chef Cristoforo di Messisbugo published a recipe for 'yellow rice' called *Riso alla Ciciliana* (Sicilian rice),[6] made by the servant of a Sicilian merchant emigrated to Milan. In this version, the ingredients are rice, saffron, bone marrow and *cervellata*, a typical Milanese sausage made in those days. I feature sausage in my recipe for *Risotto alla Milanese*, too, in Chapter 5.

In the 20th century, gold leaf was reinstated as an ingredient by the Milanese chef and founder of modern Italian cuisine Gualtiero Marchesi, who, in the mid 1980s, presented his 'Rice, gold and saffron' version of risotto, which used medium-grained carnaroli rice and four pieces of gold leaf. This risotto, fit for a king, worked perfectly in the ostentatious Milan of the mid 1980s, when the city's *dolce vita* and high fashion were at their peak.

Risotto alla Milanese retains its distinctiveness as a part of Milanese cuisine, and, in 2007, was granted a 'De.Co.' (*Denominazioni Comunali*), which recognizes the dish's municipal origin and celebrates its local, traditional preparation.

4 Wright, C. A. (2007) Risotto alla Milanese. [Online] Available at www.cliffordawright.com; accessed November 2011.
5 Artusi, P. (1960) *La scienza in cucina e l'arte di mangiar bene: Manuale pratico per le famiglie.* [*Science in the kitchen and the art of eating well: a practical guide for families,* Italian] 102 ed. (1st ed. Florence: self-published, 1891) Florence: Giunti Marzocco, pp. 91–92.
6 Wright, C. A. (2007) Risotto alla Milanese. [Online] Available at www.cliffordawright.com; accessed November 2011.

Secondi

Cotoletta alla Milanese **Milanese escalope**

One cannot talk about archetypal Milanese produce without referring to *Cotoletta alla Milanese* (Milanese escalope). However, the origin of this dish has been at the centre of a patriotic dispute between Milanese and Viennese food historians. Milan was under Austrian rule during most of the first half of the 19th century. It is believed that Field Marshal Radetzky – who led the Austrian troops during the Revolutionary Year of 1848 and the start of the First Italian War of Independence – first tasted *cotoletta* in Milan, sought out the original recipe and took it back to Vienna.[7] Today, the *Wiener schnitzel* (Viennese schnitzel) commonly uses pork instead of veal, which is always used in the traditional Milanese recipe. The original recipe dates back to the 12th century when, as Pietro Verri reports in his *History of Milan*, during a sumptuous yet solemn banquet hosted by the clergy at the Basilica of Sant'Ambrogio (St. Ambrose) church in Milan, a golden breaded loin of veal was served.[8]

Cotoletta is the Milanese name for this dish, derived from the French *côtolette*. It translates literally as 'escalope', while the similarly spelled '*costoletta*' means 'cutlet'. Historically, *cotoletta* was prepared using milk-fed veal sirloin on the bone, and contemporary Milanese chefs and other purists maintain that a true *cotoletta* has to be flattened, or tenderized, and the bone retained. Even so, throughout Italy, it is often cooked de-boned, and therefore looks more like escalope. My recipe on page 123 uses de-boned sirloin, for ease of cooking and so as not to deter adventurous children. An important tip for ensuring the quality of your *cotoletta* is to use the sirloin, not the haunch, of a young milk-fed calf; veal sirloin meat is very tender and of a light pink colour.

7   Ristorante La Tavernetta da Elio (2011) Cotoletta alla Milanese: curiosità. Si dice Cotoletta alla milanese o Costoletta alla milanese? [Online] Available at www.cotolettamilanese.it; accessed November 2011.
8   Verri, P. (1783) *Storia di Milano*. Available at Milan Digital Library. [Online] Available at www.digitami.it; accessed November 2011. Milan: Stamperia di Guiseppe Marelli, p. 165.

Saltimbocca alla Romana **Roman-style *saltimbocca***

Another *secondo* (main course) with traceable regional origins is *Saltimbocca alla Romana* (Roman-style *saltimbocca*), which was served at the lavish banquets the Roman nobility used to host over several days with some two hundred courses to be enjoyed by the guests.

A thin, lean veal delicacy made with a leaf of sage, a slice of *prosciutto crudo* (dry-cured ham or Parma ham) and fried with butter, *saltimbocca* travels to us through the centuries and its provenance may once again be determined through Pellegrino Artusi's *La scienza in cucina e l'arte di mangiar bene*. Introducing recipe number '222', Artusi advises: 'I ate them in Rome at Trattoria Le Venete and for this reason I can describe them well'.[9]

On 30 March 2011, during the course of writing this book, I attended the centenary commemorations of Artusi's death (30 March 1911). His work can almost be described as 'a sacred text' of Italian culture, and, through the centuries, his recipes have become part of every Italian family's heritage. *Science in the Kitchen and the Art of Eating Well* presents a national conformity never before attempted in Italian cuisine. Today, Italian fare remains distinctly regional, but Artusi's masterpiece nonetheless still draws together the variety of local ingredients and customs through a national journey upon which he embarks with his readers.

---

9   Artusi, P. (1960) Recipe no. 222. In: *La scienza in cucina e l'arte di mangiar bene: Manuale pratico per le famiglie*. [*Science in the kitchen and the art of eating well: a practical guide for families*, Italian] 102 ed. (1 st ed. Florence: self-published, 1891) Florence: Giunti Marzocco, p. 168.

Contorni

Insalata di pomodori **Tomato salad**

Say the word 'tomato' and an immediate association is made with pasta and pizza, and so, for much of the world, with the epitome of Italian cuisine. However, although Italy was the first European country to embrace and cultivate tomatoes, this fruit actually originates from South America. It is said to have been discovered in Montezuma's gardens by the Spanish conquistador Cortés, who brought it back to Spain in 1519.

It is thought that the original South American crops of tomatoes were mainly yellow, hence the name, in Italian, *pomodoro* (from '*pomo d'oro*', '*pomo*' meaning 'apple' and '*d'oro*' 'golden'), which was documented for the first time by the Sienese physician and naturalist Pietro Andrea Mattioli in 1544.

Botanically, the tomato is a fruit, but for culinary and nutritional purposes it is considered a vegetable. Widely used in many Italian dishes – raw in salads or cooked in sauces – it is cultivated in the south of the country, especially in the regions of Campania and Puglia. The historical link of these two regions with Spain began centuries ago, when the Spanish Empire ruled here. The Spanish imprint is still evident in the heritage of Baroque architecture, too, of which the city of Lecce is a splendid example, with its abundance of religious imagery, preference for rich ornates and a strict observance of the Catholic faith.

This religious devotion can be seen to spread through culinary beliefs in which bread is the symbol of Christ embodied. Home-made bread is prepared by using the *Madre* (Mother) dough, which is a fermentation starter (a yeast culture made with flour, water and honey left over a week). Bread has thus acquired a sacred place on the Italian table and is paired with almost every dish, especially in Puglia.

Tomato sauce and bread is a match made in heaven! The custom of the *scarpetta* is a 'naughty' little habit pardoned if indulged in at home with close family, but which is never to be practiced in restaurants or at someone else's house. '*Fare la scarpetta*' means to scoop up, with a piece of bread, the still-warm, rich tomato sauce that dressed the delicious pasta you have just enjoyed... The quality of an excellent tomato sauce is almost measured, by Italians, by how irresistible it is to scoop up the last bit of sauce left on the plate.

The simplicity of the *contorno Insalata di pomodori* (Tomato salad) – made with ripe tomatoes and basil doused with extra-virgin olive oil and sprinkled with sea salt flakes – emphasises the versatility of tomatoes, which can be enjoyed in so many ways. My version of the classic *Insalata Caprese* (*Pomodori al Formaggio Condito*) (page 82) proves it!

Formaggi

Parmesan cheese is another famous actor in the Italian performance of 'eating well and plenty'. A classically versatile Italian product, parmesan happily stands by a cold glass of Prosecco at dusk when Italians gather in bars for *l'aperitivo* (aperitifs). Half a parmesan cheese wheel sits on the bar counter, ready to be cut with its special knife and savoured by people who stand around nibbling, drinking and chatting before heading home or going to a restaurant for dinner.

Italians may begin their dinner with a starter that includes parmesan, such as *carpaccio*. They will almost certainly have a *primo* – a pasta or risotto dish – topped with a pile of grated parmesan. They may also order a *secondo* (main course) and a *contorno* (side dish) that see parmesan listed as one of the ingredients. The meal can be completed by a plate of parmesan, pears and walnuts, in place of a sweet dessert. I have not yet encountered a dessert made with parmesan, but I have tasted *gelato* made of Gorgonzola cheese combined with a scoop of pear *gelato* served in a fragrant waffle cone. A real delicacy!

Parmesan (in full, Parmigiano-Reggiano DOP) has a long history, dating back to the mid 13th century, while Grana Padano DOP,[10] another Italian hard cheese, is thought to have its origins in the 12th century. Both are produced from the milk of cattle grazing in the vast *Pianura Padana* (Po Plain), both are shaped in the form of a large wheel, and both have a similar grainy texture and a fruity or nutty flavour, depending on how long the cheese has been matured for. In spite of these similarities, however, the regional producers of each cheese assert a clear distinction through the use of the DOP designation, which is modelled on the French AOC (Appellation d'Origine Contrôlée) and which guarantees the specific origin and traditional methods of production for each cheese.

Granone Lodigiano (or Tipico Lodigiano), another 'grana' cheese, is thought to be the 'ancestor' of Grana Padano. First produced in the Middle Ages by Cistercian monks in the Chiaravalle Abbey, north of the province of Lodi, this cheese is today produced by only four dairies following the traditional methods.[11] Thanks to the hard work of the monks, who reclaimed the land around the *Val Padana* (Po Valley), within *Pianura Padana*, the region's fertile pastures led to its cows producing an abundance of milk, which was preserved through the monks' new type of cheese.

North of the Po, Grana Padano was, and still is, made using only the milk of Italian Holstein-Friesian cows. Because of the particularity of this milk, Grana Padano is low in fat and high in protein. A young wheel of Grana Padano, with 9 to 16 months of ripening, has a sweet tangy flavour, a pale colour and a grainy texture, which becomes more prominent, due to a richer presence of protein crystals, in a more mature wheel (16 to 20 months). By this stage, the cheese will have a golden colour and a nutty flavour.

Parmigiano-Reggiano is primarily produced to the south of the Po, in the region of Emilia-Romagna. Its origins date back to the mid 13th century, to the cloisters of the Cistercian and Benedictine monasteries where, again, the monks' expertize with agriculture led to surplus milk being preserved through what was to become 'the king of cheeses'. Its grainy texture, intense yet sweet flavour, fruity aroma and firm appearance are well known and appreciated worldwide. Matured for between 12 and 30 months, the wheels of Parmigiano-Reggiano are checked by professional cheese testers after 12 months, and then given a pin-dot grade selection mark according to aging time. Parmigiano-Reggiano that has been aged for more than 18 months is, with its fruity flavour, ideal for *aperitivi* and snacks. After 22 months, the cheese acquires a nuttier flavour, which becomes even more intense when it has been matured for 30 months or more.

There are more than 400 dairies that still follow the traditional method of making this cheese using just raw milk, salt, natural milk enzymes and calf rennet. Even the rind is free of additives – and entirely edible. Try cooking it wrapped in foil on a crackling fire in winter.

10 Denominazione d'Origine Protetta (in English, Protected Designation of Origin (PDO)) status.
11 LaLudesana (2009) Tipico Lodigiano cheese. [Online] Available at www.laludesana.com/products.php; accessed November 2011.

Dolci

Monte Bianco **Mont Blanc**

It is now time for us to choose a dessert to simulate our interest as well as our taste buds. Associated with agricultural practices is the dessert *Monte Bianco* (Mont Blanc), featured in Chapter 6, which, in Italy, is traditionally made on 11 November to celebrate St. Martin's Day and the end of the so-called *Estate di San Martino* ('Saint Martin's Summer', also known as 'Indian Summer'), or short period of mild autumnal weather occurring after the first frost. The dessert is particularly popular in the north Italian regions of Lombardy and Piedmont, perhaps because of its French influence. Its name is evidently Franco-Italian inspired, linked as it is to the well-known, snow-capped mountain in the Graian Alps (*Alpi Graie*).

Saint Martin of Tours (*San Martino di Tours*) is, among other attributions, patron saint of wine-growers and wine-makers, and, on St. Martin's Day in Italy, it is customary that barrels of new wine are tasted and ready to be sealed. Chestnuts, generally abundant in this season, accompany the wine tasting and are prepared in many different ways – one of which being our menu's Mont Blanc.

During the *Estate di San Martino*, agricultural contracts traditionally came to an end, and seasonal workers moved on to other opportunities. Saint Martin is commonly associated with rural communities and the migrant workers who travel through them, and the agricultural background to Saint Martin's Day is the subject of a famous poem by Nobel Prize-winner Giosuè Carducci (1835–1907), reproduced and translated on page 68 of this book for your enjoyment.

San Martino (Saint Martin)
by Giosuè Carducci

La nebbia a gl' irti colli
(Drizzling, the fog)
piovigginando sale,
(the steep hills climbs,)
e sotto il maestrale
(and the northwest wind torments)
urla e biancheggia il mar;
(the howling, foaming sea:)

ma per le vie del borgo
(but in the village streets)
dal ribollir de' tini
(the seething vats send forth)
va l'aspro odor de i vini
(the pungent smell of wine)
l'anime a rallegrar.
(and cheer the weary souls.)

Gira su' ceppi accesi
(On fiery logs the roast)
lo spiedo scoppiettando;
(turns on its spit and crackles;)
sta il cacciator fischiando
(the hunter stands and whistles)
sull'uscio a rimirar
(and watches from his door)

tra le rossastre nubi
(the flocks of birds that)
stormi d'uccelli neri,
(back upon reddish clouds,)
com'esuli pensieri,
(like forlorn thoughts gyrate)
nel vespero migrar.
(at dusk, preparing to migrate.)

Baker, J. *San Martino* by Giosuè Carducci. English trans. featured on *John Baker's blog: Reflections of a working writer and reader*, 19 March 2008. [Online] Available at www.johnbakersblog.co.uk/giosue-carducci; accessed November 2011.

Panettone

Romance leads us to sweetness, and sweetness to another Milanese cake, *panettone*. This dessert's provenance is the stuff of legends, two of the most credible of which hark back to the court of Ludovico Maria Sforza, Duke of Milan – and one of which is a love story. Ughetto degli Antellari, a Milanese nobleman and the Duke's hawk breeder, falls in love with Adalgisa, the daughter of a local baker. Various misfortunes befall the baker's family, and Ughetto, wishing to get closer to Adalgisa, offers himself as baker's assistant. The family business is falling into ruin, so, to help rejuvenate it and to receive approval from the baker, Ughetto creates a sweet bread loaf made with eggs, butter, sugar, citron peel and raisins. This speciality bread, made in the shape of a dome, was sold just before Christmas as a new celebratory cake, and immediately found success and favour. The baker's business was saved, he approved of his future son-in-law and they all lived happily ever after!

The other popular legend from the same period takes us to Christmas Eve celebrations at the *Castello Sforzesco* (Sforza Castle) in Milan. In court banquets of the time, *pâtisserie* (pastries) played an important role in demonstrating the grandeur of the hosts. That night, though, the master chef had burnt dessert... To save the chef's head, a scullery boy called Toni timidly approached his master and offered him a dessert that he had made with what was left from the dough of the dessert the chef had prepared and then burnt. The dessert that Toni had made for himself and his friends looked like a large bun with a golden crust, a fragrant aroma of fresh, sweet, buttery bread flavoured with citron peel and sultanas. The master chef decorated and presented the 'bun' to the court. The duke and duchess were pleasantly surprised by this novelty, an enthusiasm shared by their guests. After a little while, the truth came out and the '*Pan de Toni*' – as the cake was called, '*pan*' meaning 'bread' in Milanese dialect and Toni being the name of the scullery boy – became the celebrated Christmas cake, *panettone*.

Gelato

I have enjoyed *panettone* filled with *gelato*, and it is this divine combination that ends our menu of miscellany and musings. You will see that I have not translated the word '*gelato*' here, not for any patriotic or stylistic reason, but simply because I believe there to be significant differences between *gelato* and ice cream. Ice cream is generally industrially produced, it is often made with long-life ingredients and contains more fat and less of a genuine flavour than *gelato*. *Gelato*, at least as far as Italians are concerned, is the real thing and we have been enjoying it, or a very similar treat, since Roman times! (In fact, its history may even be traced as far back as ancient Egyptian civilizations.) Properly made, by artisans, *gelato* uses only natural ingredients, contains less fat and boasts higher nutritional values than its industrially made counterpart, ice cream.

'*Gelato*' means 'frozen' in Italian. Slaves were sent to the mountains surrounding Rome to collect snow to prepare cold refreshments made of fruit, snow and honey for the nobles. With the fall of the Roman Empire in the West in 476 AD, *gelato* got lost in the darkness of the Middle Ages. The Renaissance, however, rediscovered the joy of indulging into this delicious treat at the court of Caterina de' Medici. When Caterina married Henry II of France, she brought Italian *gelato* with her to the French court.

The first *gelato*-making for the de' Medici court in Florence is often attributed to either the court's architect and director of festivities Bernardo Buontalenti or a Florentine street vendor food historians identify as 'Ruggieri', thought to have gone to France with Caterina.[12] The latter story continues with Ruggieri, tired of being scorned and threatened by the French chefs at court for not revealing his recipe, fleeing France, leaving a note for Caterina explaining that he was escaping with his life but leaving behind, for her, his secret recipe for *gelato*. A frenzy of *gelato*-making ensued, with the court's chefs dedicating themselves to the art of creating this superb delicacy.

Another Italian was soon implicated, however: a Sicilian called Francesco Procopio dei Coltelli, who turned *gelato* from an exclusive delicacy for the royal court into a treat for the French aristocracy and wealthier tiers of society. In 1660, he opened the eponymous Café' Procope in Paris, which still exists today, and made it a hub for the aristocracy and literary circles.

Following in Procopio's successful steps, many other Italian *gelato* artisans emigrated north, south and west, taking along with them the tradition and skills first acquired in Italy. The ones who moved south, with its hot climate, specialized in *sorbetto* (sorbet), a type of *gelato* made of a fine balance between sugar, fruit – mainly lemon, orange and the newly introduced pineapple – and ice. Those who emigrated north to Germany and England took advantage of the abundance and quality of milk in those countries to make a creamy *gelato*. The artisans who crossed the Atlantic, going west, brought both. In Italy, Naples became both the capital of *gelato*-making and of its consumption.

Gelato arrives in England in 1672 at the court of Charles II. Due to the scarcity of ice, though, it would take two centuries for *gelato* to become established as a popular treat nationwide.

In 1851, Jacob Fussell, Jr, a milk dealer, opened the first American ice cream factory and ice cream soon became popular in every corner of the USA, alongside its ancient artisan cousin *gelato*. Even *gelato* is by now an affordable product, and it becomes 'street food' thanks to an Italian emigrant from Belluno who invented the waffle cone (*cono* in Italian) in 1903. Before the *cono*, take-away gelato was wrapped in paper and called 'hokey pokey', a play on the Italian '*ecco un poco*', which means 'here is a little'. For *gelato* lovers, 'a little' is never enough, though!

Our imaginary meal has come to an end. Having travelled through Roman banquets and royal courts and celebrated local harvests and exclusive delicacies, we now return to our times and to our tables. I have been both inspired and delighted by these stories and others like them, and have drawn as much pleasure in feeding my mind and my soul as I have in feasting on good food. Whenever I discover a historical insight or local legend, I will share it with my family and friends as we gather together around our kitchen table and savour the foods to which these facts relate and rejoice in authentic Italian tastes and traditions. No togas or corsets are required as dress code at our dinner parties, though!

12 Davies, E. Who was the real genius behind gelato? *The Florentine*, issue no. 143/2011, 19 May 2011. [Online] Available at www.theflorentine.net; accessed November 2011.

Ricette

Every day an inspiring recipe

Recipes in this chapter are presented as *antipasti* (starters or appetizers), *primi* (first course pasta, rice or other grain dishes), *secondi* (main dishes), *contorni* (side dishes) or *dolci* (desserts) as this time-honoured sequence of *portate*, or courses, in Italy is practically sacred! Some dishes are easy and quick to prepare during busy weekdays and evenings; others can be reserved for when you all have a little bit more time to set aside and enjoy preparing and eating the meal together. You can choose between serving a starter and a side dish for a light lunch or a slightly larger portion of the same starter for a more substantial meal. The black olive pâté listed as an *antipasto* following, for example, could equally well dress pasta and thus become a *primo* or first course dish.

Some of the ingredients featured are staple items and ever present in an Italian pantry and fridge, such as pasta, rice, grains, pulses, flour, breadcrumbs, tomato passata, olives, preserved tuna fillets, extra-virgin olive oil, balsamic vinegar or glaze, parmesan, ricotta, butter, eggs, cured meats, fresh fruit and vegetables – especially tomatoes, broccoli, spinach, carrots, onions, garlic and lettuce. Stock up your freezer with skinned fish fillets bought fresh from the fishmonger, skinned chicken breasts, peas, homemade soups and tomato sauce. Liven up your kitchen counter or windowsill with a pot filled with fresh herbs and edible flowers mixed together to use in your cooking and please all of your senses.

Healthy eating does not only relate to the quality and freshness of the food we consume, but also to the quantity. Moderation regarding portions and the frequency with which we eat rich foods both play an important role in maintaining a healthy family lifestyle and a positive attitude towards eating well and in good company. Throughout this book, recipes are categorized according to whether they are suitable for adults and children, adults and adventurous children or adults only. The few 'adults only' dishes, such as *Bocconcini al Vermouth* (Pork morsels in Vermouth) on page 128, generally either include small amounts of alcohol or, as with *Involtini di pollo con mortadella, caciotta e rosmarino* (Stuffed chicken breasts with mortadella, caciotta and rosemary) on page 121, are prepared using alcohol. In hot dishes such as these, most of the alcohol will evaporate through the cooking process, but the taste may still be challenging for younger palates. However, in cold dishes, such *Pesche al vino rosso* (Peaches in red wine) on page 155, the alcoholic content remains and so common sense and cultural sensitivity should prevail when considering the age at which it is appropriate for older children and young adults to enjoy such 'adults only' fare.

With almost all of these traditional, hearty, family recipes, you can simply add or remove one or two ingredients and you will be sure to please every palate, from your little ones to your guests at a Sunday lunch or a dinner party. One meal is cooked and enjoyed by all the family, leaving more time to chat, catch up and explore tastes and flavours together sitting around the table.

Antipasti

Mozzarella in Carrozza

Fried Mozzarella

Suitable for children and adults
Preparation time: 15 minutes
Cooking time: 6 minutes
Serves 4 people

What you need
4 × 200 g / 7⅛ oz / 1¾ US cups mozzarella balls
100 g / 3½ oz / ⅘ US cup white plain / all-purpose flour
1 small bunch flat-leaf parsley, finely chopped
2 whole eggs, lightly beaten
200 g / 7 oz / 1¾ US cups breadcrumbs, dry
a pinch / ¹⁄₁₆ tsp salt
sunflower oil (to fry)

How you make it
Slice the mozzarella into 16 slices, each approximately 1 cm (½ in) thick. Place the slices in a colander over a bowl to drain the milk. Save the milk in the bowl and put to one side. Using a sheet of kitchen paper / paper towel, press the mozzarella to squeeze any remaining milk out.

Put the flour on a tray or plate. Placing one slice of mozzarella at a time on the plate, dab it with flour each side.

Finely chop the parsley and put to one side.

Beat the eggs and fold the chopped parsley in.

Put the breadcrumbs in a bowl. Put the floured slices of mozzarella in the eggs and then in the breadcrumbs on both sides. Repeat twice.

Heat a generous amount of sunflower oil in a frying pan to deep-fry the mozzarella. Fry the slices for 2 to 3 minutes each side. Drain on a few sheets of kitchen paper then serve hot with a green leaf salad.

Versatility
For a slightly more elaborate version of this easy-to-prepare dish, stuff the mozzarella with mushrooms and / or *prosciutto cotto* (Italian cooked ham) to create *Mozzarella in carrozza ripiena di funghi e / o prosciutto cotto*, the recipes for which follow, and are sure to delight more adventurous diners!

Mozzarella in Carrozza Ripiena di Funghi e / o Prosciutto Cotto

Fried Mozzarella Stuffed with Mushrooms and / or Ham

Suitable for adults and adventurous children
Preslicesparation time: 25 minutes
Cooking time: 20 minutes
Serves 4 people

What you need
For the Mozzarella in carrozza:
Use the same ingredients and quantities as for *Mozzarella in carrozza* recipe on page 78.

For the filling(s):
250 g / 9 oz / 3 US cups chestnut mushrooms, cleaned and finely sliced
60 ml / 2 fl oz / 4 tbsp extra-virgin olive oil
2 whole cloves garlic, peeled
3 small to medium shallots, peeled and finely sliced
1 bunch flat-leaf parsley, roughly chopped
10 cl (100 ml) / 3½ fl oz dry white wine
freshly ground black pepper
8 slices *prosciutto cotto* (or substitute with cooked ham)

How you make it
Prepare the mozzarella slices using the method given in the recipe for *Mozzarella in carrozza* on page 78.

Clean the mushrooms by brushing them – especially the underside, to remove any dirt – then cut them into thin slices.

In a frying pan, heat the extra-virgin olive oil and add the garlic cloves, shallots, flat-leaf parsley and mushrooms. Cook on a medium heat for 5 minutes.

Add the wine, turn the heat down and cook for a further 15 minutes, stirring occasionally, until the liquid has evaporated and the mushrooms are coated and reduced in size. Add black pepper according to taste.

Take the mushrooms out and drain them in a bowl, keeping the cooked juice to one side.

Following the *Mozzarella in carrozza* recipe on page 78, dab the mozzarella slices with flour on both sides.

Place one teaspoon of mushrooms and / or a half or a quarter of the ham slice (depending on how big it is) between two floured slices of mozzarella and press firmly, especially around the edges, to form a 'parcel'. Flour your hands, if necessary, to avoid the mozzarella breaking or sticking to your hands.

Put the mozzarella parcel in the beaten eggs and then in the breadcrumbs, both sides. Repeat twice.

Deep-fry the mozzarella parcel, both sides, in a generous amount of sunflower oil. When the mozzarella has turned a golden colour, drain it on kitchen paper and serve hot accompanied by a green leaf salad.

Versatility
For a more intense flavour, use smoked scamorza (*scamorza affumicata*) cheese, available from Italian delis or good-quality supermarkets.

Tortino di Carciofi

Artichoke Omelette

Suitable for adults and adventurous children
Preparation time: 15 minutes
Cooking time: 30 minutes
Serves 4 people

What you need

6 artichokes, cleaned, trimmed and with
    'choke' removed
½ lemon
1 clove garlic, peeled and chopped
1 bunch flat-leaf parsley, finely chopped
45 ml / 1½ fl oz / 3 tbsp extra-virgin olive oil
250 ml / 8 ½ fl oz / 1 US cup water
4 eggs
120 g / 4 ¼ oz / ½ US cup parmesan cheese, grated;
    plus an extra handful, shavings
salt
freshly ground black pepper, if desired

How you make it

Clean the artichokes by cutting the stem and peeling the outer leaves off until you get to the tender inner leaves. Trim the top of the leaves and the bottom part of the artichoke. Scoop out the furry 'thistle' bit (choke) from its centre. Place the artichokes in a bowl filled with water and the lemon half until ready to use. This prevents the artichoke from turning a dark, almost black colour.

Chop the garlic. Wash and finely chop the flat-leaf parsley and set to one side.

Cut the artichokes into thick slices and put them in a large frying pan with the garlic, half of the parsley, the olive oil, the water, a pinch of salt and some freshly ground pepper (to your taste). Cover with a lid. Start cooking on a medium heat until the water boils. Turn the heat down and cook on a low heat for a further 20 minutes until the juice has thickened and the artichokes have softened.

Take the artichokes out of the pan. Drain any excess water and squeeze some of the juice out of the artichokes. Put the artichokes back in the pan.

Beat the eggs, then add the parmesan cheese, salt and pepper (to taste) and half of the remaining chopped flat-leaf parsley. Mix well.

Pour the egg mixture over the artichokes and cover with a lid. Cook for a further 3 to 5 minutes, until the egg mixture has set.

Lay the tortino on a serving plate. Sprinkle with the remaining parsley, a handful of parmesan shavings and serve hot. Add freshly ground black pepper if desired.

Versatility

An alternative serving suggestion would be to cut the tortino into individual portions and accompany each with a small, thin, toasted slice of crusty bread dressed with a dash of extra-virgin olive oil and a pinch of salt along with a green leaf salad tossed with salt, extra-virgin olive oil and some lemon juice (to taste). To serve the tortino as a light lunch, simply make larger portions of toasted bread and salad.

Pomodori al Formaggio Condito
Vine Tomatoes Stuffed with Italian Herbs and Soft Cheese

This is the classic *Insalata Caprese* (Caprese salad) revisited, in that soft creamy cheeses – such as tangy robiola, mild and creamy ricotta or full-flavoured stracchino – replace the traditional mozzarella. You could also use all of these cheeses, so that if you are preparing a buffet meal, for example, you can offer variety to your family and other guests.

I invented this recipe one late spring day, when the weather suddenly turned from warm and sunny to a little chilly. The combination of the warmth of the baked tomato with the freshness of the just-picked salad soon enlivens one's senses!

Suitable for children and adults
Preparation time: 20 minutes
Cooking time: 20 minutes
Serves 4 people

What you need
4 medium ripe vine tomatoes
a pinch of salt
30 ml / 1 fl oz / 2 tbsp extra-virgin olive oil
120 g / 5 oz robiola cheese or 150 g / 5 oz ricotta cheese
    or 120 g / 5 oz stracchino cheese (or substitute with
    other flavourful soft cheeses)
¼ tsp dry oregano
4 large leaves fresh basil, torn
1 bunch green lettuce

Optional (suitable for adults and adventurous children):
8 pitted olives (green or black, according to taste)
2 fillets anchovies (for ricotta cheese version)
1 tsp salted capers (for ricotta cheese version)

How you make it
Pre-heat the oven to 180°C / 350°F / Gas Mark 4.

Wash and pat dry the tomatoes. Using a sharp knife, slice the tops of the tomatoes off and take the pulp out. Make sure all the juice is drained. Add a little salt to the inside of the tomatoes and brush the outside with some olive oil. Pour a few drops of olive oil inside the tomato.

In a bowl, mix the cheese with the oregano and the basil.

If you are using them, slice the olives and add these to the mixture.

Spoon some of the cheese mixture into each tomato in turn.

If desired, when making the ricotta cheese version, top each tomato with a small piece of the anchovy fillet and a few capers, rinsed under cold running water to remove the salt.

Place the tomatoes in a muffin tray, to hold them in place, and put in the oven for 20 minutes. Once the skin of the tomatoes starts turning wrinkly, the tomatoes are cooked. Take them out of the oven.

Wash and then tear the lettuce. Dress the leaves with salt and extra-virgin olive oil. If you wish, add a drizzle of balsamic vinegar glaze / balsamic reduction, according to taste.

Serve the tomatoes warm on a bed of dressed lettuce.

Insalata Tiepida di Ceci e Pomodori

Warm Chickpea and Tomato Salad

This salad works for winter and summer meals and can be served as a starter and also as a light and nutritious lunch or as part of a buffet for a party. If you wish to use tinned chickpeas / canned garbanzo beans instead of dry ones, choose a good quality organic brand, which should retain their firm texture.

Suitable for children and adults
Preparation and cooking time: varies, depending on whether you are using dry or tinned (canned) chickpeas (garbanzo beans)
Serves 6–8 people (antipasti or buffet food),
  4–6 people (primo)

What you need

250 g / 8 oz dry chickpeas / garbanzo beans or
  500 g / 17 oz tinned chickpeas / canned garbanzo
  beans, rinsed and drained
1 large red onion, peeled and finely sliced
1 celery stalk, trimmed and left whole
1 carrot, peeled and left whole
4 leaves fresh sage
1 bay leaf
2 medium vine ripe tomatoes, roughly chopped
½ bunch flat-leaf parsley, roughly chopped
45 ml / 1½ fl oz / 3 tbsp extra-virgin olive oil
a dash of salt
1–3 cloves garlic, peeled and finely sliced, if desired
170 g / 6 oz meli-melo tomatoes
  (cherry and baby plum mix), whole
freshly ground white pepper, if desired
chilli pepper flakes, if desired
paprika (*dolce* / sweet)
8 large leaves fresh basil, torn

Before you cook the chickpeas / garbanzo beans:
If using dry chickpeas / garbanzo beans, soak them in cold water for 8 to 10 hours. If using tinned / canned pulses, cook directly from the tin / can. In either case, rinse and drain the chickpeas / garbanzo beans before cooking.

How you make it

Put the chickpeas, onion slices, celery stalk, carrot, sage leaves and bay leaf into a medium saucepan. Cover with cold unsalted water (three times the amount of chickpeas / garbanzo beans). Put on a medium heat and bring to the boil. When the water reaches boiling point: if using dry chickpeas / garbanzo beans, turn the heat down and gently cook for a further 50 minutes, until they are tender but still retaining their firm texture; if using tinned chickpeas / canned garbanzo beans, turn the heat down and gently cook for 10 minutes.

Meanwhile, dress the roughly chopped tomatoes and parsley with one tablespoon of olive oil and a dash of salt. Mix and set to one side.

When the chickpeas are cooked, take the celery, carrot, sage leaves and bay leaf out. Add a pinch of salt. Drain the chickpeas and onion mixture and place in a large frying pan.

Add the remaining oil, the chopped tomatoes, the flat-leaf parsley and the garlic. Mix for a couple of minutes on a medium heat until the chickpeas are coated with the oily tomato dressing. Add the whole tomatoes, stir, cover with a lid. Turn off the heat and leave to rest for 2 to 3 minutes, until the skins of the tomatoes start to wrinkle. Place in a serving bowl, adding some more olive oil and season with salt and freshly ground white pepper, chilli pepper, paprika and the fresh basil leaves. Add a little extra-virgin olive oil and mix before serving.

Versatility

You can turn this vegetarian dish into a seafood option by adding 400 g / 14 oz peeled king prawns (big shrimps) to the dressed, chopped tomatoes mixture. Leave to marinate, and then cook all together.

Be generous with the garlic: 2 to 5 cloves, finely sliced. Be liberal with the chilli pepper and sweet paprika, too, if you like strong flavours. Be even more adventurous by adding ground dry lemon peel and 5 pink peppercorns, crushed.

Carpaccio di Pesce Spada

Swordfish Carpaccio

Suitable for adults and adventurous children
Preparation time: 15 minutes
Marinating time: 30 minutes
Serves 4 people

What you need
200 g / 7 oz fresh swordfish fillet / steak
    (sustainably sourced)
1½ lemons, freshly squeezed juice of
salt
60 ml / 2 fl oz / 4 tbsp extra-virgin olive oil
2 fennel bulbs, cleaned and finely sliced
freshly ground black pepper

How you make it
Wash the swordfish fillet. Using a sharp knife, slice the fish into very thin slices. Lay on a serving plate. Pour the freshly squeezed lemon juice over the fish. Add a pinch of salt and some of the olive oil.

Remove the outer leaves of the fennel bulb. Finely slice the inner tender leaves and lay them on the fish. Pour over the remaining olive oil and sprinkle with another pinch of salt. Add freshly ground black pepper, if desired.

Leave to marinate in the fridge for 30 minutes and then serve.

Versatility
Adjust the amount of lemon according to your taste. The longer you leave the carpaccio to marinate, the stronger the flavour will be.

Carpaccio di Manzo con Rucola e Scaglie di Parmigiano

Beef Carpaccio with Rocket and Parmesan

To make this carpaccio, use either raw, very thinly sliced, extra lean beef or *bresaola*, which is air-dried salted beef. Here, the beef slices are dressed with lemon, extra-virgin olive oil, parmesan shavings and fresh salad leaves.

Suitable for children and adults
Preparation time: 15 minutes
Serves 4 people

What you need
1 lemon, freshly squeezed juice of
45 ml / 1½ fl oz / 3 tbsp extra-virgin olive oil
salt
200 g / 7 oz tender and extra lean beef, finely sliced
100 g / 3½ oz / scant 1 US cup parmesan, freshly grated
70 g / 2½ oz / 3 US cups rocket / arugula leaves
freshly ground black pepper

How you make it
Squeeze the juice of one lemon and mix with the olive oil and a pinch of salt. Pour the mixture on each layer of the beef, which is laid evenly on the serving plate. Sprinkle the grated parmesan cheese onto the beef.

Wash the rocket / arugula salad, pat dry and add to the beef.

Add freshly ground pepper, if desired, and serve.

Versatility
Experiment with adjusting the dressing to your own taste. For example, toss the rocket / arugula salad with a tablespoon of olive oil and a pinch of salt before adding it to the beef.

Carpaccio di Bresaola

Bresaola Carpaccio

Bresaola della Valtellina is air-dried, salted beef from a mountainous area in the Lombardy region of the north of Italy. It has a distinctive, salty taste and it makes a wonderful carpaccio. It can also be enjoyed with fresh goat's cheese and a squeeze of lemon on a slice of bread.

Suitable for children and adults
Preparation time: 15 minutes
Serves 4 people

What you need
200 g bresaola (or substitute with beef prosciutto)
1 lemon, freshly squeezed juice of
45 ml / 1½ fl oz / 3 tbsp extra-virgin olive oil
100 g / 3½ oz / scant 1 US cup parmesan, shavings
1 celery stalk, trimmed and finely sliced
freshly ground black pepper, if desired

How you make it
On a serving plate, arrange one layer of bresaola and pour some of the lemon juice and the olive oil over it. Continue layering and dressing until all of the bresaola has been used.

Shave the parmesan and sprinkle it on top of the bresaola.

Wash the celery and peel off its 'string'. Slice it, cutting it diagonally, and add it to the bresaola.

Grind some black pepper over the top of the carpaccio, if desired, and serve immediately.

Crostoni al Pomodoro

Tomato Crostoni

Crostoni are very simple to make and ideal for the whole family to enjoy. To emphasize this dish's versatility, I have chosen both this recipe, which accentuates the full flavour of the fresh tomatoes, and, in the following recipe, a more sophisticated combination of radicchio with creamy Gorgonzola cheese.

It is incredible what you can create with a slice of bread – even stale bread! Indeed, this recipe first came about through making good use of old bread by toasting it and then adding extra-virgin olive oil and salt for flavour… and went on to develop into numerous variations, including the two featured here.

Suitable for children and adults
Preparation time: 10 minutes
Cooking time: 5 minutes
Serves 4 people

What you need
4 slices white crusty bread or spelt (*farro*) bread
1 whole clove garlic, peeled
90 ml / 3 fl oz / 6 tbsp extra-virgin olive oil
4 medium, ripe vine tomatoes, roughly chopped
salt
1 tsp dry oregano
8 fresh basil leaves, torn
freshly ground black pepper, if desired

Optional (suitable for adults and adventurous children):
4 fillets anchovies in extra-virgin olive oil

How you make it
Pre-heat the oven to 200°C / 400°F / Gas Mark 6.

Rub the peeled clove of garlic on the crusty bread. (With younger or less adventurous palates in mind, this recipe uses just 1 clove of garlic for 4 slices of bread. However, you can increase this to up to 1 clove of garlic per slice of bread if you really are a garlic lover or do not have any pressing social engagements!)

Pour a spoonful of extra-virgin olive oil on each slice of bread. Toast in the oven for 5 minutes, turning the bread over once.

Meanwhile, chop the tomatoes and tear the basil leaves. Dress the tomatoes with salt, oregano and the basil.

Take the bread out of the oven. Top it with the dressed tomatoes. Drizzle half a tablespoon of extra-virgin olive oil over each crostone. If desired, season with freshly ground pepper.

For additional, adventurous variety, lay one fillet of anchovy atop each crostone!

Versatility
If using Italian bread for the crostoni, try *pane Pugliese, pane Toscano* or *casereccio al farro*.

Crostoni al Radicchio e Gorgonzola

Radicchio and Gorgonzola Crostoni

Suitable for adults and adventurous children
Preparation time: 15 minutes
Cooking time: 10 minutes
Serves 4 people

What you need
150 g / 5 oz Gorgonzola
300 g / 11 oz radicchio / red chicory, finely sliced
120 ml / 4 fl oz / 8 tbsp extra-virgin olive oil
2 tbsp balsamic vinegar
a pinch of salt
4 slices white crusty country bread or spelt (*farro*) bread

Optional:
walnut halves / pieces

How you make it
Pre-heat the oven to 200°C / 400°F / Gas Mark 6.

Take the cheese out of the fridge and leave to soften at room temperature.

Wash and pat dry the radicchio and cut it into thin slices.

In a frying pan, heat 4 tablespoons of extra-virgin olive oil. Add the radicchio and cook for 5 minutes on a medium heat. Add the balsamic vinegar and let the radicchio cook for another 5 minutes until it is coated. Turn the heat off, add a pinch of salt, stir well and leave in the pan to one side.

Pour 1 tablespoon of extra-virgin olive oil on each slice of bread. Put the bread in the oven and toast for 5 minutes turning once. Take the bread out of the oven.

Top the bread with the radicchio and the Gorgonzola.

Serve warm. If desired, add walnuts as an accompaniment

Versatility
If you are not too keen on Gorgonzola cheese, or blue cheese in general, you can easily substitute it with parmesan or Asiago cheese (available from delis or high-quality supermarkets). If using parmesan, slice it with a peeler and place it on top of the radicchio.

If using Asiago, dice it into small cubes. After toasting the bread for 5 minutes, add the radicchio and the Asiago cheese. Return the crostoni to the oven until the cheese melts.

Mousse al Prosciutto

Prosciutto Mousse

Suitable for children and adults
Preparation time: 10 minutes
Serves 6 people

What you need
250 g / 9 oz *prosciutto cotto* (or substitute with cooked ham)
300 g / 10½ oz ricotta cheese
a pinch of salt

Optional:
100 g / 3½ oz toasted pistachio nuts, shelled
freshly ground black pepper, if desired

How you make it
Using a food processor, cut up the ham. Add the cheese
and the salt.

Whizz at medium speed for 1 minute until the mousse
is smooth.

With a mortar and pestle, grind the pistachio nuts and add
to the mousse, if desired. Add some ground black pepper,
if desired.

Serve the savoury mousse as a delicious dip for breadsticks
and raw vegetables, such as carrots, celery, cucumber,
fennel, romaine (cos) or little gem lettuce and peppers, or
as a topping on bread and crackers. It can be served as a
starter or a healthy snack.

Mousse al Formaggio

Cheese and Chives Mousse

Suitable for children and adults
Preparation time: 10 minutes
Serves 6 people

What you need
300 g / 10 ½ oz cream cheese or fresh goat's cheese
200 g / 7 oz ricotta cheese
1 small bunch fresh chives

Optional (suitable for adults and adventurous children):
1 clove garlic, peeled and crushed
pink peppercorns

How you make it
In a food processor, blend the cheeses (along with the garlic
and pink peppercorns, for those feeling adventurous!).

Add the chives and whizz for 1 minute until the mousse
is smooth.

Serve as a dip with raw vegetables, such as fennel,
carrots, cucumber, celery, romaine (cos) or little gem
lettuce, peppers and breadsticks, or as a topping for
crackers and bread. It can be served as a starter or a
healthy snack.

Uova in Zuppa

Egg in Soup

This recipe goes back a couple of generations. My grandfather passed it down to my mother and my mother to me. I have this picture in my mind of *nonno* Pietro (granddad Peter) and his mid-morning breakfast on a Saturday. He loved relaxing playing solitaire, if on his own, or, if with his grandchildren, he would dare us to a game of cards, which we knew – and he knew – he was going to win anyway! After all this 'hard work', it was time for something to eat, as lunch wouldn't be served before half past one. He would boil the water, have the last game of cards and then gather us around the table to enjoy *uova in zuppa*.

This filling and warming dish can be served as a starter followed by a main course or just enjoyed as a main for lunch. I made it for the first time for my husband on a sunny but very cold day in Tuscany, when, during the writing of this book, the recipe suddenly came to my mind. I hadn't eaten the dish for 26 years, yet that day, for no particular reason, I recalled it. I tried hard to remember all of the ingredients and began to put the dish together, but there was still something missing… Where we were in Tuscany was pretty isolated – no telephone line or mobile reception – but I was determined to get it right and savour that distinctive taste again, so I marched halfway up the hill to where mobile phone calls still crackle but you can just about make out what the other person is saying. I phoned my aunt Paola in Milan, who revealed the missing ingredient to be grated parmesan on the sliced bread, the ultimate inclusion of which led to comforting reminiscences of childhood pleasures and time spent with *nonno* Pietro.

Suitable for children and adults
Preparation time: 5 minutes
Cooking time: 15 minutes
Serves 4 people

What you need

4 cloves garlic (reduce to 2 cloves, if preferred), peeled and sliced
1 small bunch flat-leaf parsley
16 Pomodorino tomatoes (or substitute with baby plum or cherry tomatoes)
1 litre / 34 fl oz / 4¼ US cups water
8 peppercorns
a pinch of coarse sea salt
100 g / 3½ oz / scant 1 US cup parmesan, grated
4 slices crusty bread (white, sour dough or spelt bread)
120 ml / 4 fl oz / 8 tbsp extra-virgin olive oil
4 eggs
a pinch of table salt
freshly ground pepper, if desired

How you make it

Peel and slice the garlic. If you adore garlic, do not slice it too thinly; if you or your guests are not so keen on it, though, cut really thin slices.

Wash the flat-leaf parsley and leave it whole (stalks and leaves).

Wash the tomatoes.

Pour three-quarters of the water into a very large frying pan (with a lid, which will be used later). Add the garlic, the parsley, the tomatoes, the peppercorns and a pinch of coarse sea salt. Cook for 15 minutes at medium heat. Add the remaining water when the water starts evaporating. (If you do not have a large frying pan, split all the ingredients in half, and, when you reach the relevant stage, cook the eggs two at a time).

Meanwhile, grate the parmesan cheese.

Cut 4 slices of bread and toast them in a toaster on a medium setting. When done, cut each slice of bread in half and place 1 piece each in 4 pasta bowls. Keep the other toasted halves back to be drizzled with 1 tablespoon of extra-virgin olive oil and a pinch of salt and served at the side of each of the plates on which the pasta bowls will be presented.

Sprinkle the grated parmesan generously over the 4 slices of bread lying in the bowls.

Crack the eggs over the boiling broth, lower the heat, cover with a lid and cook until the egg white starts to harden and the yolk is still runny (approximately 3 minutes).

When the eggs are cooked, gently lift them out using a big serving spoon and place one egg in each bowl on top of the bread slice.

Scoop up the broth, including the parsley, tomatoes and the garlic and share it out between the 4 bowls. Pour 1 tablespoon of extra-virgin olive oil over each egg. Season with salt and pepper. Serve hot with the other half slice of bread, drizzled with oil and a pinch of salt, at the side of the plate.

Versatility
If using Italian bread, try *pane Pugliese*, *pane Toscano* or *casereccio al farro*.

Paté di Olive

Olive Pâté

In general, children tend to like olives because of their salty flavour. Given the choice, green olives are preferred to black because they are sweeter and do not have that bitter after taste often found in black olives. I have chosen here pâté recipes using both so that you can decide if one is tastier than the other after all!

You can use both the black and green olive pâtés as crostoni toppings or as a dip for *grissini* (breadsticks) and raw chopped vegetables, such as carrots, fennel, celery, romaine (cos) or little gem lettuce, cucumber, peppers and tomatoes. Black olive pâté can also be used to dress pasta, as noted in the 'Versatility' section below.

Paté di Olive Nere
Black Olive Pâté

Suitable for adults and adventurous children
Preparation time: 10 minutes
Serves 8 people

What you need
300 g / 11 oz black olives, pitted and chopped (baked olives are best if you can find them)
1 clove garlic, peeled and chopped
90 ml / 3 fl oz / 6 tbsp extra-virgin olive oil
1 tsp dry oregano

How you make it
In a blender, chop the olives and the garlic. Add 4 tablespoons of extra-virgin olive oil and the oregano. Blend at medium speed for 1 minute.

Pour the mixture in a glass jar / ceramic container and cover with the rest of the extra-virgin olive oil.

This *paté di olive nere* will stay fresh stored in the fridge for three days. Make sure the pâté is always covered with extra-virgin olive oil. Add a couple of spoonfuls of oil to the jar when necessary.

Paté di Olive Verdi
Green Olive Pâté

Suitable for children and adults
Preparation time: 10 minutes
Serves 8 people

What you need
300 g / 11 oz green olives, pitted and chopped
1 clove garlic, peeled and chopped
90 ml / 3 fl oz / 6 tbsp extra-virgin olive oil
1 tsp fennel seeds (optional)

How you make it
Use the same method as for the *paté di olive nere*, adding the fennel seeds in this recipe last if you wish to use them.

Serve as a topping for crostoni or as a dip for *grissini* (breadsticks) and fresh raw chopped vegetables.

Paté di olive verdi will stay fresh in the fridge for up to three days. As with the other pâté, make sure that it is always covered with extra-virgin olive oil and top up the jar with oil if necessary.

Versatility
The pâté can also be used as a sauce to dress spaghetti. Use it as is, or add it to the pasta with some roughly chopped tomatoes, a few leaves of fresh basil and a couple of tablespoons of olive oil, resulting in a very quick and easy way to prepare a *primo*!

Primi

Bucatini con Sugo di Fagiolini e Ricotta Salata

Bucatini with Tomato Sauce, Green Beans and Mature Salted Ricotta

This is another of my grandfather's favourite recipes – he was an excellent cook and it was his passion for food that my mother inherited and then passed on to me. He would often serve this dish followed by *triglie* (red mullet) and then peaches in red wine or lemon syrup (*see* page 155) as a fresh and flavourful meal for us all to enjoy.

If the *ricotta salata* (also known as *ricotta dura* or hard ricotta) is too strong a flavour for younger palates, substitute it with parmesan cheese. As a child, I used to love *ricotta salata*, though, precisely because it is so-o-o salty and tangy!

Suitable for children and adults
Preparation time: 20 minutes
Cooking time: 15 minutes
Serves 4–6 people

What you need
3½ litres / 118 fl oz / 14¾ US cups water
1 large onion, peeled and chopped
2 cloves garlic, peeled and chopped
90 ml / 3 fl oz / 6 tbsp extra-virgin olive oil
1 tbsp water
500 g / 16 fl oz tomato passata
5 g / 1 tsp (half a palmful) coarse sea salt
350 g / 12 oz bucatini pasta (or substitute with fusilli bucati, which is also hollow, or mafalde)
250 g / 9 oz French beans / green beans, trimmed
a few leaves of fresh basil, torn
salt
pepper
150 g / 5¼ oz / 1½ US cups *ricotta salata* cheese, grated (or substitute with Pecorino Romano *stagionato*, or mature Pecorino Romano)

How you make it
In a large saucepan, bring the water to the boil.

Chop the onion and the garlic.

In another large pan, put 4 tablespoons of olive oil, 1 tablespoon of water, the onion and the garlic on a low to medium heat and gently simmer. Add the passata and simmer for 15 to 20 minutes.

While the tomato sauce simmers, add the sea salt to the boiling water and cook the pasta according to the instructions detailed on the packaging or until *al dente*.

Wash the green beans and put them in to boil with the pasta for the last 7 to 10 minutes of cooking time, depending on the thickness of the green beans you are using and also how tender you like them.

Wash and dry the basil leaves, then tear them into pieces using your hands. Add the basil to the tomato sauce once you've turned the heat off and stir in.

Grate the *ricotta salata* cheese with the grater (big holes). Depending on the consistency of the cheese, you may be able to crumble it with your hands.

Drain the pasta and the green beans. Add the tomato sauce. Sprinkle with the *ricotta salata* and mix well. Serve immediately. Add freshly ground black pepper to taste.

Versatility
Combining fresh ricotta, rather than *ricotta salata*, with the tomato sauce provides a more delicate taste and creamier texture and gives the cooked sauce a pinkish tinge.

Pappardelle alla Crema di Peperoni

Pappardelle with Red Romano Pepper Sauce

This is one of my family's favourite *primi*. I have also cooked the dish many times for Sunday lunch for friends with children and we have all enjoyed the sweetness of the long, thin, red Romano peppers. For the adults' version, you could spice up the dish by adding some chilli pepper.

Suitable for children and adults
Preparation time: 15 minutes
Cooking time: 20 minutes
Serves 4 people

What you need

3½ litres / 118 fl oz / 14¾ US cups water
4 Romano peppers (or substitute with red bell peppers), deseeded and sliced
2 medium onions, peeled and chopped
1 clove garlic, peeled and crushed
1 bunch fresh chives, chopped
75 ml / 2½ fl oz / 5 tbsp extra-virgin olive oil
2 tbsp water
1 tsp dry Italian herbs
salt
black pepper, freshly ground
5 g / 1 tsp (half a palmful) coarse sea salt
200 g / 7 oz single / light cream (or mascarpone cheese)
350 g / 12 oz pappardelle (or substitute with fettuccine)
50 g / 1¾ oz / ½ US cup parmesan, grated
50 g / 1¾ oz / ½ US cup Pecorino Romano, grated (or substitute with 100 g / 3½ oz / scant 1 US cup parmesan, total)

How you make it

Bring water to the boil in a large pasta saucepan.

Wash the peppers, cut them in half, take the seeds out and cut them into thin slices.

Chop the onion and crush the garlic.

Chop the chives and keep to one side.

Put the olive oil, water, onions, garlic, peppers, dry herbs, salt and pepper in another saucepan and cook on a low to medium heat for 10 minutes, stirring occasionally.

By now, the pasta water should have reached boiling point. Add the sea salt. Add the pappardelle and cook it for approximately 7 minutes, or until *al dente*. (Follow the instructions listed on the packaging.)

Returning to the sauce, when the peppers and onions are soft, add the cream / mascarpone cheese and cook the sauce for a further 5 minutes.

Serve the drained pasta out into bowls, pour the sauce over it and mix well. Sprinkle the grated cheese and the chives over the top of each dish and serve immediately.

Add freshly ground pepper if desired.

Versatility

For a vegetarian version of this dish, substitute parmesan or Pecorino Romano with an alternative Italian hard cheese, such as *Pecorino con caglio vegetale*, that is made using vegetable rennet.

Farfalle, Zucchine, Mascarpone e Zafferano

Farfalle with Courgettes, Mascarpone and Saffron

The delicate flavour of this pasta dish is sure to please everybody. The peak season for courgettes / zucchini is May to August, so you have spring and summer to enjoy this dish.

Suitable for children and adults
Preparation time: 15 minutes
Cooking time: 15 minutes
Serves 4–6 people

What you need
3½ litres / 118 fl oz / 14¾ US cups water
1 large onion, peeled and finely sliced
2 cloves garlic, peeled and finely sliced
4 medium courgettes / zucchini, sliced
45 ml / 1½ fl oz / 3 tbsp extra-virgin olive oil
1 tsp dry oregano
a pinch of salt
220 g / 7½ oz mascarpone cheese
150 g / 5¼ oz / 1½ US cups parmesan cheese, grated
5 g / 1 tsp (half a palmful) coarse sea salt
a generous pinch of saffron
350 g / 12 oz farfalle (also known as 'bow tie' pasta)
black pepper, freshly ground

How you make it
Bring the water to boil in a large saucepan.

Finely slice the onion and garlic.

Wash and then, using the grater (big holes), grate the courgette / zucchini. Or, if you have a food processor, julienne the courgettes / zucchini into long thin strips.

Pour the extra-virgin olive oil into a large frying pan. Add the onions and the garlic and cook at a low heat for 5 minutes, until the onions are soft and golden. Add the courgettes / zucchini and the oregano and simmer for another 10 minutes, stirring occasionally. Add a pinch of salt, the mascarpone cheese and the parmesan, stir well and, when the mixture has combined, turn the heat off. Keep the sauce warm. If you think that the sauce is a bit too thick, add a spoonful or two of the water from the large saucepan to it.

When the pasta water reaches boiling point, add the sea salt, then add the saffron, which will flavour and colour the pasta to a bright yellow. Add the pasta and cook according to the packet's instruction or until *al dente*.

Drain the pasta and toss it into the frying pan with the sauce to flavour.

Serve immediately.

Grind some black pepper over the top, if desired.

Versatility
Substitute the mascarpone with either ricotta, for a lighter version, or with stracchino / *crescenza* cheese, for a full, round flavour. The latter is delicious, even though not exactly slimming, but well worth an extra work out in the gym or a long walk after lunch!

Penne dell'Estate

Summer Penne

This pasta dish can be eaten hot or at room temperature on a sizzling summer day. It is a *primo* but can equally well be part of a barbeque or a buffet menu. If your children are not keen on aubergines / eggplants, simply pick these out of the dish once cooked. That way, they can enjoy the rich flavour of the aubergine / eggplant without having to deal with its texture.

Suitable for children and adults
Preparation time: 20 minutes
Cooking time: 20 minutes
Serves 4 people

What you need
3½ litres / 118 fl oz / 14¾ US cups water
5 g / 1 tsp (half a palmful) coarse sea salt
1 large aubergine / eggplant, cut into small cubes
1 bunch spring onions, finely sliced
2–3 cloves garlic (according to taste), peeled
    and chopped
250 g / 1 ball mozzarella cheese, drained and diced
½ bunch fresh basil, torn
4 fresh San Marzano tomatoes (or substitute with another
    variety of plum tomato), diced
75 ml / 2½ fl oz / 5 tbsp extra-virgin olive oil
a pinch of salt
a pinch of dry oregano
1 sprig fresh thyme
30 g / 1 oz / 5 tbsp fresh breadcrumbs
350 g / 12 oz penne (dry)

Optional (suitable for adults and adventurous children):
1 tbsp black olive paste / tapenade
2 fillets salted anchovies, rinsed and chopped
black pepper, freshly ground
30 ml / 1 fl oz / 2 tbsp extra-virgin olive oil
fresh chilli pepper

How you make it
Bring the water to boil in a large saucepan. Add the sea salt.

Wash and dice the aubergine / eggplant into small cubes. Wash and finely slice the spring onion. Peel and chop the garlic. Dice the mozzarella cheese and set to one side. Wash and tear the basil leaves.

Blanch the tomatoes in the salted boiling water for one minute. Remove and then peel away the skin. Dice the tomatoes and set to one side.

In a large saucepan (with a lid, to be used later), pour the olive oil, add the garlic, a pinch of salt, the oregano, the thyme and the breadcrumbs and simmer for a few minutes, stirring. Add the aubergine / eggplant, cover with a lid and cook for 15 minutes. In the last few minutes of cooking, add the spring onions. When the spring onions have softened a little, turn the heat off and cover the sauce with a lid.

When the salted pasta water reaches (or returns to) boiling point, add the pasta. Cook until *al dente*, according to the packet's instructions.

Drain the pasta and put it into a large serving bowl.

Add the aubergine sauce, the tomatoes and, just before serving, the mozzarella. Stir well. Add the torn basil leaves and serve hot. If served at room temperature, add the tomatoes and the aubergine sauce to the pasta, stir well and let it cool down. Add freshly ground black pepper to taste. Drizzle 2 further tablespoons of extra-virgin olive oil, if desired, before serving.

Optional (suitable for adults and adventurous children):
Add the black olive paste / tapenade to the sauce. Rinse the anchovies under cold running water, to remove the excess salt, and chop. Mix into the sauce. Slice the fresh chilli pepper and add the quantity according to your taste.

Mix well and serve.

Orecchiette con i Broccoli

Orecchiette with Broccoli

This dish can be as mild or as full of rich Mediterranean flavour as you like – the suggested 'optional' additions to the original recipe will create a 'grown-up' flavour for adults and adventurous children alike.

Suitable for children and adults
Preparation time: 15 minutes
Cooking time: 20 minutes
Serves 4 people

What you need
250 g / 9 oz broccoli florets
3½ litres / 118 fl oz / 14¾ US cups water
5 g / 1 tsp (half a palmful) coarse sea salt
350 g / 12 oz orecchiette (domed disc-shaped pasta)
60 ml / 2 fl oz / 4 tbsp extra-virgin olive oil
black pepper

Optional (suitable for adults and adventurous children):
2–3 cloves garlic, peeled and crushed
2 bread rolls, centres scooped out (for breadcrumbs)
75 ml / 2½ fl oz / 5 tbsp extra-virgin olive oil,
    plus extra for drizzling
black pepper, freshly ground to your taste
½ tsp crushed red peppercorns

How you make it
Wash the broccoli florets and set to one side.

Bring the water to the boil in a large saucepan. When the water reaches boiling point, add the sea salt and the pasta.

Cook the pasta according to its packet instructions or until *al dente*. In the last 5 to 7 minutes of cooking, add the broccoli to the water.

Drain the pasta and the broccoli, keeping a little of the cooking water to one side.

Dress with the extra-virgin olive oil and, if desired, the black pepper, mixing well. Some of the broccoli will crumble, forming a sauce with the olive oil. If the dish looks a bit dry, add 1 tablespoon at a time of the set-aside cooking water until moist. Mix well, add black pepper if desired and serve.

To add a touch of full Mediterranean flavour to this dish, you can dress the orecchiette slightly differently, as follows.

Optional (suitable for adults and adventurous children):
Drain the pasta and broccoli, retaining some of the cooking water as before.

Crush 2 to 3 cloves of garlic. Remove the soft part of the bread roll and crumble. Pour 5 tablespoons of extra-virgin olive oil into a large saucepan and put it on a low heat. After a couple of minutes, when the oil is hot, add the garlic and the breadcrumbs. When these turn a golden colour, add the pasta and the broccoli and stir well for one minute to allow the sauce to soak into the pasta.

Drizzle with olive oil and sprinkle with the crushed red peppercorns and a generous amount of black pepper. Serve immediately.

Fusilli al Sugo di Tonno

Fusilli Pasta with Red Tuna Sauce

Pasta, passata, tuna fillets preserved in extra-virgin olive oil in jars and olives are always present in an Italian pantry. These ingredients will come in handy for making a quick complete pasta meal for supper any day of the week when you are pressed for time, or it can be prepared for Sunday lunch as part of a menu. The sauce is rich, dense and flavoured with herbs. This dish was tested by six children and by five adults on a Sunday, when it was eleven of us sitting around our kitchen table… This pasta, along with the red, white cabbage, carrots and orange salad, and the apples in a parcel were part of the menu I cooked for my family and friends. Everything was cooked and eaten in between a mid-morning coffee, biscuits and a good catch up, and an after lunch walk in the woods. We wanted to do it all… so three simple recipes to enjoy both the company of friends and good healthy food.

Suitable for children and adults
Preparation time: 15 minutes
Cooking time: 20 minutes
Serves 4–6 people

What you need

4 litres / 135 fl oz / 17 US cups water
3 medium onions, peeled and thinly sliced
2 garlic cloves, peeled and thinly sliced
½ small bunch fresh chives, chopped
½ small bunch fresh flat-leaf parsley, chopped
300 g / 11 oz green and black pitted olives, drained
300 g / 11 oz tuna fillets (sustainably sourced) preserved in
    extra-virgin olive oil, drained
700 g / 1 lb 9 oz passata (sieved tomatoes)
200 ml / 6¾ fl oz / ¾ US cup water
½ tsp dried Italian mixed herbs
10 g / ½ tbsp (a palmful) coarse sea salt
400 g / 14 oz fusilli
    (or substitute with tortiglioni rigati pasta)
60–90 ml / 2–3 fl oz / 4–6 tbsp extra-virgin olive oil
black pepper, freshly ground

Optional:
200 g / 7 oz fresh garden peas
dry chilli flakes (or powder)

How you make it

In a large pot, bring the water to the boil.

Thinly slice the onions and the garlic. Chop the chives and the flat-leaf parsley. Drain the olives. Weigh the tuna once it is drained of the extra-virgin olive oil in which it is preserved to check you are using the correct amount. I use tuna fillets that are preserved in extra-virgin olive oil in jars. Whichever you choose, make sure the quality of the tuna fillets is good because this will determine the taste of your sauce.

Put all of these ingredients in a large casserole. Add the tomato passata. Pour the 200 ml / 6¾ fl oz / ¾ US cup of water into the tomato passata bottle, close the top of the bottle and shake it. You will not only free up any passata left in the bottle, and so not waste any, but you will also have the right amount of water to dilute the passata a little. Finally, add the teaspoon of dry herbs and stir all the ingredients together. Put the casserole on a low heat and simmer for 20 minutes, stirring occasionally.

When the pasta water boils, add the coarse sea salt, then the pasta and cook until *al dente*, according to the packet instructions. For fusilli pasta, 11 minutes usually suffices, especially if you are mixing the pasta into the simmering sauce once it has been drained, as you will be doing for this recipe.

Drain the pasta and drizzle a little extra-virgin olive oil over it, so that it does not stick, and gently stir.

Check, by tasting, that the onions in the sauce are soft. If so, at this stage (after about 20 minutes), the sauce is ready. Keep it on the low heat, gently stir the pasta in and continue to cook for a couple of minutes. Turn the heat off. Pour as many tablespoons of olive oil as the number of your portions (4 to 6) and gently stir. Serve immediately, either in a big serving pasta bowl or as individual portions. Season with freshly ground black pepper (to taste) and, if desired, dry chilli flakes (or powder).

Optional:

If you are adding the peas to the sauce, add them towards the end, let's say 4 to 5 minutes before turning the heat for the sauce off, so that they cook but retain their firm texture.

Spaghetti con le Vongole o Cavatelli con Vongole Rucola e Grana

Spaghetti with Clams or Cavatelli with Clams, Rocket and Parmesan

This is a variation on a dish I have enjoyed at the previously discussed Ristorante Lo Sfizio, where chef Gina transforms the classic *Spaghetti con le vongole* (Spaghetti with clams) into a delicacy using cavatelli, a type of pasta shaped like small curled-up shells and which originates from southern Italy. If you can find fresh cavatelli, for example, in an Italian deli, do try this recipe 'Sfizio style'. Spaghetti is the pasta traditionally used, though, and I have used it here as 10-year-old Hester – one of the stars of this book, who you will meet again in later chapters – loves *Spaghetti con le vongole* and the more clams, the better!

Suitable for adults and adventurous children
Preparation time: 20 minutes
Cooking time: 15–20 minutes
Serves 4 people

What you need
2–3 cloves garlic (to taste), peeled and crushed
2 fresh San Marzano tomatoes (or substitute with another variety of plum tomato), chopped
1 bunch flat-leaf parsley, chopped
1 kg (2 lb) fresh live clams / *vongole* (with their shells)
4 litres / 135 fl oz / 17 US cups water
30 ml / 1 fl oz / 2 tbsp extra-virgin olive oil
20 cl (200 ml) / 7 fl oz dry white wine
200 ml / 6¾ fl oz / ¾ US cup hot water
5 g / 1 tsp (half a palmful) coarse sea salt
400 g / 14 oz fresh cavatelli (or substitute with dry spaghetti)
salt
white pepper, to taste
chilli pepper, to taste

Optional:
200 g / 7 oz / 8½ US cups rocket / arugula
100 g / 3½ oz / scant 1 US cup parmesan, shavings

How you make it

Chop the garlic, the tomatoes and the parsley and keep to one side in separate bowls. Thoroughly wash the clams in cold running water and, once clean of any possible sand residue, keep to one side.

For the pasta, bring the water to boil in a large saucepan. Into a very large, non-stick frying pan, pour the olive oil, add the garlic and slowly fry on a low heat for a few minutes, paying attention not to burn the garlic.

Put the clams in the frying pan (with a lid, to be used later), add the white wine and turn the heat up to medium. Stirring with a wooden spoon, cook the clams until the wine evaporates, then add 200 ml / 6¾ fl oz / ¾ US cup of hot water. Cook the clams until they open. Discard any that do not open whilst cooking (clams that don't open are 'off').

Add the chopped tomatoes to the clams and cook for a further couple of minutes. Cover with a lid, turn the heat off and leave the clams to rest.

Meanwhile, when the water in the saucepan has reached boiling point, add the sea salt and then the pasta. If you are using fresh cavatelli, cook it for 6 minutes. If you are cooking dry spaghetti, follow the packet instructions to cook until *al dente.*

Drain the pasta. Turn the heat back on the frying pan and mix the pasta in with the clams. If necessary, add a little bit more warm water to moisten. Stirring constantly, mix well for a couple of minutes, and then turn the heat off.

Serve the pasta on a large serving plate. Another of Gina's modern interpretations of the traditional dish is to add the 'optional' rocket / arugula and parmesan shavings at this point, too. Whichever version of *pasta alle vongole* you have created, dress it with 2 tablespoons of extra-virgin olive.oil and finely chopped parsley. Season with salt, white pepper and, if desired, chilli pepper.

Fagiolata

Bean Soup

Bean soup is linked to an old traditional agricultural ritual for when the land needed rain. In the open countryside, a large cauldron was put on the boil with beans, various other pulses and salt-cured meat. While the soup was boiling, the diners were sprayed with water to invoke rain.

A warming and comforting food, rain or shine, this is a vegan / vegetarian version of the classic dish, which usually includes pancetta (Italian bacon) or pork sausages. If you would like to reintroduce a touch of meat to my recipe, have a look at the tip included below.

Bean soup can be prepared hours in advance and then simply re-heated before serving.

Suitable for children and adults
Preparation time: 20 minutes
(plus 8–12 hours of pre-soaking time for the beans)
Cooking time: 65–70 minutes
Serves 4–6 people

What you need
250 g / 1¼ US cup mixed dry beans
    (such as cannellini, borlotti, kidney beans, black-eyed
    peas / beans and black beans / black turtle beans)
1½ litres / 51 fl oz / 6⅓ US cups cold water
1 large onion, peeled and finely sliced
1 garlic clove, peeled and finely sliced
3 plum tomatoes, chopped
1 large potato, peeled and paper-thinly sliced
1 celery stick, chopped
1 medium carrot, peeled and chopped
½ small bunch flat-leaf parsley, chopped
2–3 sprigs fresh thyme (or ½ tsp dry thyme)
2–3 (depending on size) leaves fresh sage
4 black peppercorns, crushed
a drizzle of extra-virgin olive oil
salt
chilli pepper, dry (optional)

How you make it
Soak the beans in cold water for 8 to 12 hours, then discard this water and rinse the beans in cold running water.

Put the beans into a large saucepan (with a lid, which will be used later) and pour 1½ litres / 51 fl oz / 6⅓ US cups of cold water over them.

Peel and finely slice the onion and the garlic. Chop the rest of the vegetables and add everything to the beans. Wash, chop and add the parsley. Then add the thyme and the sage.

Bring the bean soup to the boil on a medium heat. When it boils, cover with a lid and cook on a low heat for a further hour until the beans are soft. In the last 5 minutes of cooking time, add the crushed peppercorns.

When the soup is cooked, season with salt (to taste) and stir.

Serve hot with a drizzle of extra-virgin olive oil over each bowl. For the adults, add a sprinkle of dry chilli pepper, if desired.

Versatility
To make a meaty bean soup, fry ½ tablespoon of extra-virgin olive oil and one large onion, finely sliced, with 100 g / 3 oz of diced pancetta (available from Italian delis or good-quality supermarkets), a sprig of fresh rosemary and a few leaves of sage. Gently fry for 3 to 4 minutes until the onion is soft and golden in colour. Remove the rosemary and the sage. Put this mixture into the saucepan you will be cooking the beans in and proceed with the rest of the recipe as above.

Farro e Verdure al Salto

Tossed Farro and Vegetable Salad

Suitable for children and adults
Preparation time: 30 minutes
Cooking time: 30 minutes
Serves 4–6 people

What you need
1 large red onion
150 g / 5¼ oz green beans, trimmed
200 g / 7 oz / 1½ US cups *farro*
    (or substitute with bulgur wheat)
1½ litres / 51 fl oz / 6⅓ US cups warm water, salted
½ tsp fennel seeds (optional)
2 medium continental salad onions (or substitute with
    4 small spring onions), chopped
1 yellow bell pepper, roughly chopped
1 red bell pepper, roughly chopped
2 medium courgettes / zucchini, roughly chopped
150 g / 5¼ oz baby plum tomatoes
    (or substitute with cherry tomatoes), halved
½ bunch flat-leaf parsley, roughly chopped
½ bunch fresh chives, roughly chopped
1 sprig fresh oregano (or ½ tsp dry oregano)
90 ml / 3 fl oz / 6 tbsp extra-virgin olive oil
salt
black pepper, freshly ground

Optional:
200 g / 7 oz caciocavallo dolce cheese, shavings
    (or substitute with a caciotta, pecorino or scamorza type
    cheese, fresh or smoked, according to your taste and
    what is available)

How you make it
Peel the onion, leave it whole and set to one side.

Wash, top and tail the green beans and set to one side.

Put a large saucepan on a medium to high heat for one minute. Put the *farro* in and toast it, stirring constantly for 1 minute. Pour the salted warm water into the saucepan, add the large red onion and the fennel seeds (if desired). Cook on a low heat for 20 minutes or until *al dente*. In the last 5 to 10 minutes of cooking, depending on their thickness, add the green beans.

Meanwhile, wash, clean and chop the rest of the vegetables. Set the tomatoes, parsley and chives to one side.

Once the *farro* is cooked, drain then run it under cold water to separate the grains. Put the *farro* and the green beans in a large serving bowl and set to one side.

Pour 3 tablespoons of extra-virgin olive oil into a large pan and add the oregano and a pinch of salt. Add the salad / spring onions, courgettes / zucchini and bell peppers, tossing the vegetables with a wooden spoon. Cook for 10 minutes on a medium heat, stirring and checking that the vegetables do not burn. In the last 5 minutes of cooking, add the tomatoes and stir well.

Stir the vegetables into the *farro* and the green beans. Add the parsley and the chives. Dress with the remaining olive oil and season with salt and pepper to your taste.

Optional:
Using a peeler, shave the cheese and add it to the *farro* and vegetables once cooking is completed.

Risotto

Risotto

Originally the staple diet of northern Italy, risotto is nowadays celebrated and enjoyed all over the world.

There are three principal types of rice with which to make risotto. The variety perhaps most commonly used, at least by Italian families, is Arborio, which is a rounded, short-grained rice cultivated in the plains of Lombardy. It is easy to cook and, in fact, doesn't really overcook. Vialone, from the Veneto region, produces a lighter risotto with the cooked grains being quite moist, soft and creamy. Venetian risottos are cooked *all'onda*, which is to say a little 'wave' of cooking juice is created when spooning the risotto. Finally, Carnaroli, a medium-grained rice that can be found in Piedmont, is considered to be premium-quality risotto rice. It has a distinctive flavour, retains a firm texture and cooks uniformly, absorbing a generous amount of the cooking stock.

The 'Italian secret' to making an excellent risotto is the final, *mantecatura* stage. To *mantecare* the risotto means to remove it from the heat, add a knob of butter (thereby making it even 'creamier'), stir and then let the risotto rest, covered with a lid, for 2 minutes before serving it.

If your first risotto is anything but perfect, don't despair, as, when it comes to making risotto, practice really does make perfect! All of the risotto recipes that follow have been tried and tested across the generations in my family, as have the other recipes featured in this book, and so you are sure to find success with them, too!

Risotto Bianco Cremoso

Creamy White Risotto

The recommended rice for this recipe is Vialone, as the final result should be a moist risotto. Vialone is generally widely available, but, if sourcing it does prove difficult, use Arborio rice instead, as this variety works well for all risottos.

Suitable for children and adults
Preparation time: 10 minutes
Cooking time: 18–20 minutes
Serves 4 people

What you need
1 litre / 34 fl oz / 4¼ US cups vegetable or chicken stock
   (*see* below)
2 shallots, peeled and finely sliced
100 g / 4 oz / 1 stick butter
a pinch of ground nutmeg
a pinch of salt
300 g / 10½ oz Vialone rice
10 cl (100 ml) / 3½ fl oz dry white wine (optional)

For the stock:
1 onion
1 carrot
1 potato
1 celery stick
1 litre / 34 fl oz / 4¼ US cups water
4 peppercorns
salt
chicken (optional; for non-vegetarian version)

Optional:
100 g / 3½ oz / scant 1 US cup Grana Padano, grated
   (or substitute with parmesan / vegetarian equivalent)

How you make it
Peel the vegetables for the stock. Into a medium-sized saucepan, pour the water, add the peeled vegetables (and the chicken, if desired) and bring to the boil.

Peel and finely slice the shallots. Into a casserole pan (with a lid, to be used later), put the shallots, half of the butter, the nutmeg and a pinch of salt and gently fry for 3 minutes.

Add the rice, stir and toast it for 2 minutes. Add the white wine and stir.

Add one ladleful of hot stock at a time, keep stirring and cook for a further 10 minutes.

Whilst cooking the rice, taste it to check that the grain has retained its firm texture. This means that it is cooked *al dente*. Keep the rice moist and creamy by adding stock.

Add the rest of the butter, half of the grated cheese (if desired) and stir well. Season with salt according to taste.

Turn the heat off, cover the risotto with a lid and leave it to *mantecare* for 2 minutes.

Serve hot with the rest of the grated cheese.

Versatility
The cheese is listed as optional as, without it, this risotto will have a delicious delicate flavour. While on the subject of delicate flavours, in the last 5 minutes of cooking the risotto, try adding 2 handfuls of fresh peas. Flavour and decorate with some torn leaves of fresh mint. Sublime! (This version works best served without cheese.)

Risotto con Asparagi e Gamberi

Asparagus and Prawn Risotto

Use Carnaroli rice in this risotto to match the delicacy and texture of the other ingredients. If you can't get hold of Carnaroli, though, Arborio will work just as well.

Suitable for adults and adventurous children
Preparation time: 20 minutes
Cooking time: 18–20 minutes
Serves 4 people

What you need

14 asparagus spears / shoots, trimmed
1 litre / 34 fl oz / 4¼ US cups vegetable stock (*see* below)
2 medium shallots, peeled and finely sliced
45 ml / 1½ fl oz / 3 tbsp extra-virgin olive oil
300 g / 10½ oz / scant 1½ US cups Carnaroli rice
300 g / 11 oz peeled prawns / shrimp
50 g / 1¾ oz / ½ stick butter
salt
black pepper, freshly ground

For the stock:
1 onion
1 carrot
1 potato
1 celery stick
1 small shallot
1 litre / 34 fl oz / 4¼ US cups water
4 peppercorns
salt

How you make it

Clean the asparagus and remove the thicker, woody bottom of each stem. Cut the tips off, keeping them to one side.

Peel the vegetables for the stock. Into a medium-sized saucepan, pour the water, add the peeled vegetables and a pinch of salt and bring to the boil.

When the stock reaches boiling point, dip the asparagus (without the tips) in for 3 minutes. Then scoop out the asparagus and cut it up into small pieces. Keep the stock hot, as you will be using it to make the risotto.

Finely slice the 2 medium shallots. Into a casserole, pour 2 tablespoons of extra-virgin olive oil, add the shallots and gently fry for a few minutes. Add the rice and toast for a few minutes, stirring constantly.

Add one ladleful of hot stock and let it evaporate. Keep adding one ladleful at a time, as the stock is absorbed, stirring constantly for 5 minutes.

Dip the tips of the asparagus into the stock for 2 minutes, scoop them out and set to one side. Cook further until the rice is soft but the grain still retains its firm texture (approximately 5 to 8 minutes). Towards the end of the cooking time, add the main pieces of asparagus, and then the prawns / shrimp. Cook for 3 minutes. Add the asparagus tips and stir well.

Turn the heat off, add the knob of butter, stir and leave the risotto covered with a lid to *mantecare* for 2 minutes.

Put the risotto on a serving plate, drizzle with the remaining olive oil and grind some black pepper over the top, if desired.

Versatility

For a vegetarian version of this dish, simply prepare the risotto without the prawns / shrimp and enjoy it served with some grated hard cheese, such as *Pecorino con caglio vegetale*, made with vegetable rennet (*caglio vegetale*).

Risotto alla Milanese con Zafferano e Salsiccia

Milanese Risotto with Saffron and Sausage

The recommended rice for this recipe is Arborio, a short-grain rice cultivated in Lombardy, the Italian region from where the classic recipe of *Risotto alla Milanese* originates.

Suitable for children and adults
Preparation time: 20 minutes
Cooking time: 18–20 minutes
Serves 4 people

What you need

2 shallots, peeled and finely sliced
200 g / 7 oz sausages, chopped and with skin removed
50 g / 1¾ oz / ½ stick butter
1 sprig fresh rosemary
1 sprig fresh sage
salt
pepper
300 g / 10½ oz / scant 1½ US cups Arborio rice
1 litre / 34 fl oz / 4¼ US cups stock (*see* below)
a generous pinch of saffron powder,
    plus extra saffron threads
100 g / 3½ oz / scant 1 US cup Grana Padano, grated
    (or substitute with parmesan cheese)

For the stock:
1 carrot
1 onion
1 potato
1 celery stalk
1 litre / 34 fl oz / 4¼ US cups water
4 peppercorns
salt
beef

Optional:
10 cl (100 ml) / 3½ fl oz white wine

How you make it

For the stock, peel the carrot, the onion, the potato and clean the celery stalk. Into a saucepan, pour the water, add the peeled vegetables, a pinch of salt, 4 peppercorns, the beef and bring to the boil. Once boiled, keep the stock hot.

Peel and finely chop the shallots and set to one side. Remove the skin from the sausage and cut into small pieces.

Into a casserole, put half of the butter, the chopped shallots, the rosemary, the sage, a pinch of salt and pepper and the sausages. Gently fry on a low heat until the shallots are soft and the sausage is golden (approximately 3 minutes).

Add the rice and toast it for 2 minutes. Take the sage and the rosemary out. Pour in the wine (if using) and allow it to evaporate.

Add one ladleful at a time of hot stock and cook, constantly stirring, for 10 minutes.

Add the saffron dissolved in 2 tablespoons of stock and keep cooking for further 5 to 7 minutes, adding more hot stock as necessary.

Turn the heat off, add the remaining butter, stir, cover the risotto with a lid, let it *mantecare* for 2 minutes and then serve.

Grate some Grana Padano cheese and sprinkle some saffron threads over each serving to decorate.

Versatility

Another Grana-type cheese, Granone Lodigiano (Tipico Lodigiano), is produced in the Lombardy region of Italy and is one of the ingredients in the original Lombard recipe for risotto. If you are lucky, you may find this tasty cheese stocked at an Italian deli or specialist store – if so, do try using it with the risotto recipes and enjoy a true taste of Italy!

Crema di Verdura Verde

Creamy Green Soup

This soup is real 'super food'! Beet greens (the leafy tops of beetroot; similar to chard leaves in preparation and use), kale, green cabbage, leeks and parsley contain – in varying proportions – a significant amount of vitamin A, K and C.

I make this soup very 'green' and quite thick and creamy. However, you can vary the 'greenness' of the soup by adding a potato, which will soften the taste of the other vegetables, and add as much liquid as you like to reach the thickness desired.

Suitable for children and adults
Preparation time: 20 minutes
Cooking time: 25 minutes
Serves 4–6 people

What you need
1½ litres / 51 fl oz / 6⅓ US cups water
300 g / 10 oz beet greens
200 g / 7 oz any seasonal greens, kale or green cabbage
½ small bunch flat-leaf parsley, leaves only
2–3 large potatoes, peeled and thickly sliced
    (quantity depends on how 'green' you like your soup)
1 large onion, peeled and quartered
1 large leek, trimmed and halved
a generous pinch of coarse sea salt
60–90 ml / 2–3 fl oz / 4–6 tbsp extra-virgin olive oil
55–85 g / 2–3 oz mascarpone cheese

Optional (to decorate):
black pepper, freshly ground
parmesan cheese, grated

How you make it
In a large saucepan (with a lid, used later), bring the water to the boil.

Wash the green vegetables and the parsley. Thickly slice the potatoes. Quarter the onion. Trim, wash and halve the leek.

When the water boils, add all the vegetables, cover the saucepan with a lid and cook on a low heat for 20 minutes until the potatoes are soft. Add salt to taste.

Drain the vegetables, retaining the vegetable stock. Put the vegetables in a food processor and whizz, adding – a little at a time – the amount of stock necessary to obtain the consistency of the soup desired. (I like this soup really creamy and thick.) If you don't have a food processor, you can use a hand-held mixer.

Serve hot, adding a tablespoon of mascarpone and a drizzle of extra-virgin olive oil to each bowl.

Add ground black pepper and some grated parmesan cheese if you wish.

Versatility
This green soup can be enjoyed in the springtime, too, by substituting other green seasonal ingredients, such as spinach, peas and courgettes / zucchini. Eat healthy every season of the year!

Minestrina di Pastina, Lenticchie e Verdure in Brodo

Pastina, Lentil and Vegetable Soup

This is the recipe for the much-loved *minestrina*. From childhood to adulthood, every Italian has enjoyed this hearty dish on cold winter evenings. As a family, we have either *minestrina* or vegetable soup to warm up and as a good start to the meal. If you or your children are not too keen on pulses, leave the lentils out and enjoy the *minestrina* with vegetables, chicken or both. For a vegetarian version, omit the chicken.

Suitable for children and adults
Preparation time: 20 minutes
Cooking time: 20 minutes
Serves 4–6 people

What you need

150 g / 5 oz / 1 US cup organic tinned / canned lentils, rinsed (or substitute with half the quantity of dry green lentils – *see* 'Versatility' below)
1 carrot, peeled and chopped
1 onion, peeled and chopped
1 potato, peeled and diced
1 celery stick, trimmed and chopped
150 g / 5¼ oz / 2¼ US cups cauliflower florets
150 g / 5¼ oz / 5 US cups fresh spinach
1½ litres / 51 fl oz / 6⅓ US cups water
1 bay leaf
1 sprig marjoram
a pinch of coarse sea salt
150 g / 5 oz pastina (choose from little stars, melon seeds, small circles and tiny square pasta shapes)
60–90 ml / 2–3 fl oz / 4–6 tbsp extra-virgin olive oil

Optional:
1 chicken breast

How you make it

Rinse the lentils and set to one side. Peel and chop the vegetables into small pieces.

If you are making a *minestrina* with chicken, hammer out the chicken breast and cut it into small pieces.

Fill a large saucepan with the unsalted water. If using dry lentils, put them in the water now; if using tinned / canned lentils, add them after the water has boiled. Bring the water to the boil. Add the chopped vegetables, the herbs and the chicken (if used) and cook for 20 minutes on a low heat.

Check the cooking time on the packet of the pastina you have chosen and add it at the right time accordingly.

When the *minestrina* is cooked, add salt and drizzle with extra-virgin olive oil. Serve hot.

Versatility

I prefer to use dry organic pulses, for their nutritional levels, and I favour green lentils as they do not require soaking and cook in 15 to 20 minutes, retaining a firm texture.

Secondi

Involtini di Pollo con Mortadella, Caciotta e Rosmarino

Chicken Breasts stuffed with Mortadella, Caciotta Cheese and Rosemary

Suitable for children and adults
Preparation time: 20 minutes
Cooking time: 25 minutes
Serves 4 people

This stuffed chicken breast dish used to delight me when I was a child and my girls now really like it too. Filled with creamy cheese and seasoned Italian charcuterie (mortadella or a similar product, bologna / boloney), gently roasted with rosemary and sage, this is a succulent main course to be savoured slowly and enjoyed as part of a complete, unhurried meal.

What you need

4 free-range organic chicken breasts

2–4 slices mortadella (or substitute with honey roast ham /
 cooked ham), depending on the size of the chicken breast

4 thin slices caciotta (or substitute with Fontina, Bel Paese,
 Asiago, fontal or other similarly textured cheese that
 will melt nicely; not mozzarella as it is too watery)

4 pinches dried Italian mixed herbs

4 flat-leaf parsley leaves

75 ml / 2½ fl oz / 5 tbsp extra-virgin olive oil

1 large red onion, peeled and finely sliced

1 bunch fresh rosemary

4 leaves fresh sage

salt

white pepper

thread (for cooking) or toothpicks (to tie up the chicken rolls)

How you make it

Hammer the meat out so that you have 4 thin slices
of chicken.

Lay 1 slice of mortadella and one thin slice of cheese onto
each slice of meat. Sprinkle each with a pinch of dry herbs
and add a leaf of flat-leaf parsley.

Roll the meat up as tightly as possible so that the stuffing
does not leak out whilst cooking. Use cooking thread or
toothpicks to secure.

Put the olive oil, the finely sliced onion, the rosemary, the
sage, salt and pepper into a large frying pan (with a lid, used
later) and gently fry on a low heat.

When the onion starts to soften, turn the heat up to medium,
put the chicken rolls in and cook until they start to colour.
Turn them a few times so that they colour evenly.

Turn the heat back down, cover with a lid and cook on a low
heat for another 20 minutes, turning the meat occasionally.

Season with salt, and white pepper if desired, before serving.

Optional (suitable for adults):
Crush a clove of garlic and share it equally among the filling
of each chicken breast. When braising the chicken rolls, pour
half a glass of dry white wine, dry Marsala or sherry, cover
with a lid and cook according to the recipe above.

Cotoletta alla Milanese

Milanese Escalope

Coming from Milan, I of course had to include this recipe. In fact, I have suggested three versions: the classic, below, served with no sauce, and to be enjoyed with a green salad, tomato salad, potatoes or risotto; the *Gustosa*, topped with melted Fontina cheese and speck (cured meat); and the *Cotoletta in Agrodolce* topped with an onion sauce. Choose your favourite, or just try them all!

To find a healthier option to the northern Italian *Cotoletta*, we have to travel to the most southerly part of Italy: Sicily. Here, *Cotoletta alla Palermitana* is made without eggs or flour and is baked instead of fried. To make it, mix the same amount of breadcrumbs with 1 or 2 cloves of garlic (accordingly to taste), crushed into a paste, half a small bunch of parsley (leaves only) and 50 g / 1¾ oz / ½ US cup Pecorino Romano cheese, grated. Brush the meat with extra-virgin olive oil. Dip it into the breadcrumb mixture and pat well, so that it sticks on both sides. Pre-heat a fan oven to 190°C / 375°F / Gas Mark 5. Place the *Cotoletta alla Palermitana* on a baking tray and cook for 10 minutes, until golden. Turn halfway through cooking, to obtain an even crust. Add salt to taste.

Suitable for children and adults
Preparation time: 10 minutes
Cooking time: 15 minutes
Serves 4 people

What you need

4 loins high-welfare veal (or substitute with tenderized chicken breasts)
4 eggs
100 g / 3½ oz / ⅘ US cup white plain / all-purpose flour
120 g / 4¼ oz / 1 US cup breadcrumbs, dry
a pinch of salt
80 g / 3 oz / ¾ stick butter
15 ml / ½ fl oz / 1 tbsp extra-virgin olive oil

How you make it

Hammer the meat out with a tenderizer to make it thinner.

Beat the eggs.

Dip the meat in flour, in the eggs and then in the breadcrumbs. Repeat the egg and breadcrumb coatings twice and then set to one side.

Into a large frying pan, pour the oil and add the butter and put it on a low heat. When the oil is hot and the butter has melted, fry the escalope until golden.

Drain on kitchen paper. Season with salt, to taste.

Serve hot.

Versatility

For a lighter version of this dish, replace the butter and olive oil with 8 tablespoons of sunflower oil. While frying, add more oil as necessary.

Cotoletta Gustosa

Melt-in-your-mouth Escalope

Suitable for children and adults
Preparation time: 20 minutes
Cooking time: 20 minutes
Serves 4 people

What you need

1 large red onion, peeled and sliced in rings
30 ml / 1 fl oz / 2 tbsp extra-virgin olive oil
a pinch of salt
1 tbsp balsamic vinegar
4 loins high-welfare veal (or substitute with chicken breast)
4 eggs
100 g / 3½ oz / ⅘ US cup white plain / all-purpose flour
120 g / 4¼ oz / 1 US cup breadcrumbs, dry
80 g / 3 oz / ¾ stick butter
15 ml / ½ fl oz / 1 tbsp extra-virgin olive oil
4 slices Fontina
4 slices Italian speck (or substitute with *prosciutto cotto* or honey roast ham / cooked ham)

How you make it

Set the grill on high.

Peel the onion and slice in 4 onion rings. Marinate in extra-virgin olive oil, salt and balsamic vinegar.

Hammer the meat out with a tenderizer to make it thinner.

Beat the eggs.

Dip each escalope in flour, in the eggs and then in the breadcrumbs. Repeat the egg and breadcrumb coatings twice and then set to one side.

Into a large frying pan, pour the oil and add the butter and put it on a low heat. When the oil is hot and the butter has melted, fry the escalope until golden.

Drain on kitchen paper.

Lay one slice of cheese, one slice of speck and one onion ring on each escalope. Place under the grill until the cheese melts and the speck start to crisp.

Serve hot.

Versatility

If you or your children don't like its smoky flavour, substitute the speck with *prosciutto cotto* (cooked ham). And if the thought of eating onions does not fill your little ones with joy either... you can always have two onion rings instead of one! Through the centuries, the original recipe has used butter and olive oil; for a lighter version, though, you can substitute these with 8 tablespoons of sunflower oil. Add more oil, while frying, as necessary.

Cotoletta di Maiale in Agrodolce

Sweet and Sour Pork Cutlets

Suitable for adults and adventurous children
Preparation time: 20 minutes
Cooking time: 30 minutes
Serves 4 people

What you need
4 pork cutlets
4 eggs
100 g / 3½ oz / ⅘ US cup white plain / all-purpose flour
120 g / 4¼ oz / 1 US cup breadcrumbs, dry
3 large onions, peeled and finely sliced
60 ml / 2 fl oz / 4 tbsp extra-virgin olive oil
1 fresh bunch sage
500 ml / 17 fl oz / 2 US cups white vinegar
500 ml / 17 fl oz / 2 US cups water
150 g / 5½ oz / ¾ US cup brown sugar
1 tsp salt
8 black peppercorns, ground
80 g / 3 oz / ¾ stick butter
15 ml / ½ fl oz / 1 tbsp extra-virgin olive oil

How you make it
Hammer the cutlets out to make them thinner.

Beat the eggs.

Dip each cutlet in flour, in the eggs and then in the breadcrumbs. Repeat the egg and breadcrumb coatings twice and set to one side.

Finely slice the onions. Into a large frying pan, pour the extra-virgin olive oil, add the onions and cook on a low heat until they start to soften. Add the sage and the vinegar, and cook for a further few minutes letting the vinegar evaporate. Add the water, the sugar, the salt and the pepper. Cook on a slow heat until the juice reduces to a thick sauce.

In a very large frying pan, pour the olive oil and add the butter. When the oil is hot and the butter has melted, fry the cutlets until they turn to a golden colour. Drain on kitchen paper.

Serve the cutlets dressed with the sweet and sour onion sauce.

Versatility
Although this recipe traditionally uses butter and olive oil, for a lighter version, you can substitute these with 8 tablespoons of sunflower oil. Add more oil, while frying, if required.

Polpette al Sugo

Meatballs in Tomato Sauce

This is another classic Italian dish. *Polpette* can be eaten as a main course with a side dish or, mixed with tortiglioni (pasta) and steamed peas, they make a complete meal.

One of the ingredients that gives flavour to these *polpette* is the Grana Padano cheese, which is produced in the Val Padana (Po Valley) in Lombardy – hence the name – and it is a fresher cheese than the otherwise similar parmesan, as it is matured for fewer months overall. It also has a smoother, softer texture and flavour and is less dry than parmesan, which means that it melts more easily. Grana Padano is also sublime eaten uncooked with pears and walnuts.

Enjoy these *Polpette al sugo* and the intense aroma they emanate during cooking, which will fill your kitchen and your heart with a wonderful comforting sensation!

Suitable for children and adults
Preparation time: 20 minutes
Cooking time: 20 minutes
Serves 4–6 people

What you need
1 onion, peeled
1 shallot, peeled
1 carrot, peeled
1 celery stick, trimmed
4 sprigs flat-leaf parsley, finely chopped
½ white bread roll
200 ml / 6¾ fl oz / ¾ US cup milk
a pinch of ground nutmeg
400 g / 14 oz extra-lean minced / ground beef
1 egg
a pinch of salt
80 g / 2¾ oz / ¾ US cup Grana Padano, grated
50 g / 1¾ oz / ½ US cup breadcrumbs, dry
60 ml / 2 fl oz / 4 tbsp extra-virgin olive oil
750 ml / 25⅓ fl oz / 3 US cups tomato passata
a few fresh basil leaves

How you make it
Blitz the peeled onion, shallot, carrot and celery in a food processor until a smooth mixture is formed. Set to one side.

Finely chop the parsley and set to one side.

Remove the soft part of the bread roll. Soak it in milk and nutmeg.

Into a large mixing bowl, put the minced meat, beat in the egg, add the parsley, a pinch of salt and mix well.

Squeeze the milk out of the bread and add to the meat mixture. Add the Grana Padano and mix well. Add the breadcrumbs one tablespoon at a time, gauging the consistency of the meat mixture. If it is firm enough to make meatballs that will set, do not add any more breadcrumbs, or the *polpette* may turn out too dry.

Using your hands, roll medium-sized meatballs and lay them on a plate to set.

Into a large casserole, pour 2 tablespoons of extra-virgin olive oil, add the vegetable mixture and put on a low heat. After 5 minutes, put the *polpette* gently in the casserole one at a time, making sure they do not get squashed. Cook for 5 minutes, turning the *polpette* to colour them evenly.

Pour in the tomato passata and simmer for 45 minutes on a very low heat, stirring occasionally.

When cooked, pour in the other 2 tablespoons of extra-virgin olive oil and add a few fresh basil leaves.

Versatility
As noted above, with *Polpette al sugo*, you can make a complete meal by adding pasta and peas. Simply boil the pasta and, in the last 5 minutes of cooking, add the peas. When cooked, drain. Add the *polpette* with tomato sauce, stir well, sprinkle some freshly grated parmesan cheese on top and serve hot.

Calamari alla Romana

Golden-Fried Squid Rings

Angelica – another of the stars of the book – absolutely adores this dish. Try it and see if you share her enthusiasm!

Suitable for children and adults
Preparation time: 15 minutes
Cooking time: 15 minutes
Serves 4 people

What you need
For the pastella (batter):
2 eggs
50 ml / 1¾ fl oz / ¼ US cup cold sparkling water (if cooking for children) or 50 ml / 1¾ fl oz / ¼ US cup cold beer (if cooking for adults only)
60 g / 2 oz / ½ US cup white plain / all-purpose flour
a pinch of salt

For the calamari (squid):
500 g / 16 oz calamari, cut in circles
flour (enough to coat the calamari)
abundant sunflower oil, to fry
1 lemon

How you make it
Ask your fishmonger to clean and cut the calamari into circles, ready to be fried.

Wash the calamari under cold running water and pat dry.

Dip the calamari in flour.

In a large frying pan, heat the sunflower oil.

Dip the calamari in the batter you have made by mixing all the *pastella* ingredients together. Make sure water or beer are cold as this helps bind the batter.

When the oil is hot, fry the coated calamari until they turn to a golden colour.

Season with salt and add a squeeze of lemon as desired.

Bocconcini al Vermouth

Pork Morsels in Vermouth

Suitable for adults only
Preparation time: 25 minutes
Cooking time: 15 minutes
Serves 4–6 people

What you need
100 g / 4 oz *prosciutto cotto* (or substitute with cooked ham)
500 g / 1 lb 2 oz minced / ground pork meat
1 egg
50 g / 1¾ oz / scant ½ US cup parmesan cheese, grated
50 g / 1¾ oz cream cheese
a pinch of ground nutmeg
salt
white pepper, ground
flour (to coat the morsels)
50 g / 1¾ oz / ½ stick butter
5 leaves fresh sage
25 cl (250 ml) / 8½ fl oz Vermouth

How you make it
Finely chop the ham.

Into a large mixing bowl, put the pork, the ham, the egg, the parmesan, the cream cheese, nutmeg, salt and pepper and mix well.

Using your hands, divide the mixture into small portions, rolling, shaping and patting them into round, shaped morsels. Coat the morsels with flour.

In a large frying pan, melt the butter, add the sage and fry the morsels until they turn a golden colour.

Add the Vermouth and turn the morsels so that they cook evenly for about 25 minutes.

Branzino al Cartoccio
Sea Bass Parcels

Suitable for children and adults
Preparation time: 10 minutes
Cooking time: 20–30 minutes
Serves 4 people

What you need

4 medium sea bass (line caught / sustainably sourced;
    ask your fishmonger to fillet and de-bone the fish ready
    to be baked)
4 medium potatoes, unpeeled, scrubbed, sliced paper thin
4 tsp salted capers
1 bunch flat-leaf parsley
2 lemons
60 ml / 2 fl oz / 4 tbsp extra-virgin olive oil
4 cloves garlic, whole and skin on
4 sprigs fresh thyme
4 tsp fennel seeds
coarse sea salt
8 peppercorns, ground
120 ml / 4 fl oz / 8 tbsp water (if cooking for children)
    or 12 cl (120 ml) / 4 fl oz dry white wine (if cooking
    for adults)
4 tsp pine nuts
non-stick baking sheets (baking parchment, silicone paper)
    or aluminium foil

How you make it

Pre-heat the oven to 200°C / 400°F / Gas Mark 6.

Wash the fish and place each one on a sheet of baking parchment / kitchen foil large enough to be able to wrap the fish. Prepare and wrap each fish with its condiment individually.

Scrub, wash and slice (paper thin) the potatoes. Using a steamer, steam the potatoes for 3 minutes. Remove the potatoes from the steamer, place on a plate and set to one side.

Wash the capers in cold running water and set to one side. Wash the parsley and set to one side. Cut the lemons into thin slices and set to one side.

Open each fish slightly and, in the middle, put 1 tablespoon of olive oil, 1 clove of garlic (peeled and thinly sliced), some of the parsley (whole stem and leaves), 1 sprig of thyme, 2 slices of lemon, 1 teaspoon of capers, 1 teaspoon of fennel seeds, salt and the pepper if desired. Add 2 tablespoons of water / wine per fillet.

Lay the slices of one potato and one teaspoon of pine nuts on top of each fish then dress with salt and pepper to taste. Wrap each fish in the parchment / foil and close tightly. Place the wraps together on an oven tray and bake for 20 to 30 minutes (depending on the size of the fillets), checking half way through that the fish is not overcooking.

Versatility

If you do not want to use potatoes, simply omit them as this will not affect the final dish.

Filetto di Cernia con Mandorle

Grouper Fish Fillet with Almonds

Suitable for children and adults
Preparation time: 20 minutes
Cooking time: approximately 25 minutes
Serves 4 people

What you need

1 fillet grouper (approximately 500 g /1 lb 4oz),
    whole and skinned (or substitute with cod)
1 large onion, peeled and finely chopped
3–4 cloves garlic, according to taste,
    peeled and finely chopped
150 g / 5 oz / 1 US cup chopped almonds
30 g / 1 oz / scant ½ US cup breadcrumbs, dry
½ bunch fresh basil, finely chopped
½ bunch flat-leaf parsley, chopped
½ bunch fresh chives, chopped
105 ml / 3½ fl oz / 7 tbsp extra-virgin olive oil
a pinch of salt
freshly ground Creole mix peppercorns
    (black, white, green, pink peppercorn mix)

How you make it

Pre-heat the fan oven at 200°C / 400°F / Gas Mark 6.

Chop the onions, the garlic, the basil, the flat-leaf parsley and the chives and set to one side in different bowls.

Put the fish in an ovenproof large casserole or frying pan, transferable to the oven, add salt and pour 5 tablespoons of extra-virgin olive oil over the fish.

Add the onion, the garlic, the basil, the parsley, the almonds and the breadcrumbs on top.

Cover with a lid and cook for 10 minutes on a low heat. Check occasionally, so that the fish does not stick to the pan.

Remove the lid and add 2 tablespoons of extra-virgin olive oil. Transfer to the oven and cook for further 5 to 7 minutes, depending on the thickness of the fish.

In the meantime, chop the chives.

Put the grill on medium to hot – depending on the strength of your grill – and grill for 3 to 4 minutes until the breadcrumbs are golden and a crust has formed.

When the fish is cooked, sprinkle with chives. Add the freshly ground Creole mix, if desired, and season with salt if needed.

Saltimbocca

Saltimbocca

This is a very quick and tasty dish for meat lovers.
Serve with potatoes, steamed green vegetables or a salad.

Suitable for children and adults
Preparation time: 10 minutes
Cooking time: 4 minutes
Serves 4 people

What you need
400 g thinly sliced high-welfare veal (or substitute with
    extra-lean, very thinly sliced beef)
150 g / 5 oz Parma ham, sliced
1 bunch fresh sage
toothpicks
2 cloves garlic, whole
30 g / 1 oz / ¼ stick butter

How you make it
Lay one slice, or half a slice, of Parma ham onto each slice of
meat (depending on the size of the slices of the meat and the
slices of the *prosciutto di Parma*).

Lay one leaf of sage on top and hold the layers together with
a toothpick.

By pressing it with the back of a blunt knife, crush each garlic
clove. Into a large saucepan, put the butter and the crushed
cloves of garlic and cook through on a low heat. When the
butter has melted, add the slices of meat a few at a time and
cook for 4 minutes at a medium/high heat.

Serve immediately.

Versatility
If you like sun-dried tomatoes, lay one on each slice of meat
under the sage leaf.

Frittata Verde

Green Frittata

Frittata is an Italian version of a flavourful omelette, and is just as good whether eaten warm or cold. Served warm, it can be accompanied by a fresh mixed salad to make a perfect *secondo*. Eaten cold, frittata makes an excellent picnic, a party or buffet food and can also be used as filler for *panini*.

Suitable for children and adults
Preparation time: 20 minutes
Cooking time: 20 minutes
Serves 4 people

What you need
1 medium potato, peeled and thinly sliced
1 medium onion, peeled and thinly sliced
150 ml / 5 fl oz / 10 tbsp extra-virgin olive oil
½ tsp dried Italian herbs
1 clove of garlic, peeled and chopped
2 tbsp water
4 whole eggs
50 g / 1¾ oz mascarpone cheese or ricotta cheese
    (or substitute with another soft Italian cheese, quark
    or cream cheese)
100 g / 3½ oz / scant 1 US cup parmesan, grated
350 g / 12½ oz / 11¾ US cups raw spinach,
    washed and dried
1 egg white, beaten
a pinch of salt

How you make it
Peel and thinly slice the potatoes and the onions. Put them in a non-stick frying pan with 3 tablespoons of extra-virgin olive oil, the herbs, the chopped garlic and the water and simmer for 10 minutes, until the onions are coloured and the potatoes soft. Stir occasionally.

Meanwhile, beat the eggs, add the soft cheese and stir until you have a smooth texture. Add the parmesan and stir. Add the potatoes, onions and spinach to the mixture. Fold in the well-beaten egg white last.

With some kitchen paper, wipe the non-stick frying pan you have used to cook the onions and potatoes. Pour the remaining olive oil into the frying pan. Heat the oil and, when ready, pour in the mixture. Lower the heat to low / medium. Cover with a lid and let it cook for 10 minutes. Check that the mixture sets without burning.

Now turn the frittata over, using a plate, and cook the other side for 10 minutes. Check if more frying oil is needed.

There is an easier option to cook the frittata on both sides without risking breaking it. Before you start preparing the frittata, pre-heat the oven to 180°C / 350°F / Gas Mark 4. Once the bottom side of the frittata has been cooked in the non-stick frying pan, transfer the oven-safe frying pan to the oven and bake for 10 minutes until golden and firm. Make sure you use a frying pan with a stainless steel handle, or, if it has a plastic one, wrap it in aluminium foil before transferring the pan to the oven. After 10 minutes, the frittata can be quickly grilled for a few minutes to brown the top and make it crispy.

Once cooked, sprinkle the frittata with coarse sea salt and serve warm with a salad.

Versatility
If you are not too keen on spinach, substitute it with thinly sliced courgettes / zucchini, asparagus tips or a few leaves of beet greens, which have a milder flavour. The choice is yours, depending on the season.

Torta Salata Rustica

Courgette Pie

This recipe was one of my mother's masterpieces. For us, it was a delicious lunch, dinner, snack, picnic or buffet food… we used to eat it at any time of the day, hot or at room temperature, in the winter or in the summer. One *torta salata* usually lasted only a few hours!

My mother often used to make two *torte salate* on a Sunday, knowing that the first was going to be 'just a little taster' while the second might last for another meal during the week. It keeps in the fridge for up to 4 days… if you can resist it!

The oven tin shown in the photograph is a 'family heirloom' as it is the same tin my mother used and is now more than 35 years old.

Suitable for children and adults
Preparation time: 60 minutes
Cooking time: 50 minutes
Serves 6 people

What you need
For the pasta brisé / shortcrust pastry / pie crust dough:
200 ml / 6¾ fl oz / ¾ US cup ice-cold water
500 g / 17½ oz / 4 US cups white plain / all-purpose flour, plus extra for dusting
250 g / 8¾ oz / 2¼ sticks butter, cold, diced (keep it cold), plus extra for greasing
½ tsp salt (for the dough)
a generous pinch of coarse sea salt (to dress)

For the filling:
4 medium courgettes / zucchini, finely sliced lengthways
2 medium, ripe vine tomatoes or plum tomatoes, sliced
200 g / 1 ball mozzarella cheese, drained of its water and well squeezed
½ small bunch flat-leaf parsley, finely chopped
½ small bunch basil, finely chopped
1 egg
1 egg yolk
1 tsp dry oregano

20 g / 3 tbsp / ¾ oz breadcrumbs, plus an extra handful
100 g / 3½ oz / scant 1 US cup parmesan, grated
50 g / 1¾ oz / ½ US cup pecorino cheese, grated
salt
pepper

How you make it
For pasta brisé / shortcrust pastry / pie crust dough:
Put the water in the fridge to cool, or use cold water if already stored in the fridge.

Sieve the flour onto a cold surface, such as marble or glass; otherwise, use a large glass mixing bowl. Run your hands under cold water and pat them dry. This will help to keep the pastry cool, too, while you are working it, which is important. Make a hole and add the cold cubed butter and the salt. Work the mixture quickly with your fingertips.

Take the water out of the fridge and slowly pour it onto the mixture until it becomes a sticky dough. You may not need the full amount – judge for yourself. When the dough reaches an 'elastic' consistency, stop adding water. If you have a food processor, blitz the flour and butter first until a crumbly mixture is obtained, then gradually add the water until a smooth dough is formed.

When the dough is smooth, shape it into a ball, wrap it in cling film / plastic wrap and, with the help of a rolling pin, shape it into a disc. Leave it to rest for 1 hour in the fridge.

In the meantime, prepare the filling.

For the filling:
Pre-heat the oven to 180°C / 350°F / Gas Mark 4.

Finely slice the courgettes / zucchini lengthways. Slice the tomatoes. Drain, squeeze and then slice the mozzarella. Finely chop the parsley and the basil.

Beat the egg and the egg yolk and add the fresh herbs, the dry oregano, the breadcrumbs, the grated cheeses, and the salt and pepper.

Take the dough out of the fridge. Work it lightly to soften it. Separate it into two pieces. With a rolling pin, roll out the first piece of dough onto a floured surface.

Grease a round baking tin with butter and flour it. Lay the rolled-out dough in the tin making sure that some overlaps the edge (for sealing the pie). Using a fork, make some holes in the dough.

Bake the pastry for 15 to 25 minutes, until the pastry has dried out, set and turned a pale gold colour. The exact time will depend on your oven.

Take out of the oven and leave it to stand for 5 minutes.

Sprinkle the base with an extra handful of breadcrumbs, to ensure that it doesn't become too soggy after the filling is added.

Pour in some of the egg mixture and then layer the courgette / zucchini, tomatoes and mozzarella across it. Pour in some more egg mixture. Repeat until all of the ingredients have been used.

Roll out the second piece of dough and place it on top. Seal the sides. With a fork, make a few holes in a circle. Sprinkle with coarse sea salt and put the pie into the oven.

Bake it for 30 to 35 minutes, until the pastry starts to lightly colour. Check that the top circle of pastry is cooked.

Leave the pie to cool for 5 minutes before serving if you want to eat it fresh out of the oven. Of course, you can also enjoy it cooled at room temperature…

Versatility

The *pasta brisé* / shortcrust pastry / pie crust dough can be prepared up to 2 days in advance. Store it in the fridge until you decide to make your pie. Take it out of the fridge 30 minutes before working the dough. It can also be frozen for 1 week. Defrost before using it. The pastry can be used for savoury or sweet pies. The filling may vary, too. Try spinach and ricotta cheese, for example, or be inventive with your own favourite vegetables.

If you are one of those who can't have a meal without meat, add some grilled and sliced chicken breast or some diced pancetta (Italian bacon) to the pie filling. This suggestion was made to me by the Schmidlin-Ackermans family who tried out the original recipe for me at a birthday party celebrated on a sunny Mediterranean island. Nineteen members of the family tasted the pie and all of them loved it, but some 'carnivores' suggested adding meat… an alternative version was duly made, and it worked, too!

Peperonata con Lenticchie Mielate

Honey-Drizzled Peppers and Lentil Stew

I was discussing vegetarian dishes with my vegetarian friend Angela and we both came to the conclusion that this is one of our favourites. Children love it too because of the hint of sweetness from the honey. For this recipe, I suggest green lentils, as they do not require soaking and cook quicker than other varieties, but, if you are short of time, use organic tinned (canned) lentils instead. Simply drain the lentils, mix with the cooked peppers (see below) and cook for 5 minutes. Then add the honey (or vegan alternative) and cook for a further 5 minutes.

You can make this recipe in advance and the sweetness of the honey will become more accentuated as the dish is left to rest. It can be gently reheated and served.

Suitable for adults and adventurous children
Preparation time: 20 minutes
Cooking time: 25 minutes
Serves 4–6 people

What you need

250 g / 9 oz / 1 US cup dry green lentils
1½ litres / 51 fl oz / 6⅓ US cups cold water, unsalted
2 large onions, one peeled and the other peeled
    and chopped
1 clove garlic, peeled
1 bay leaf
1 yellow pepper, sliced
1 red pepper, sliced
1 orange pepper, sliced
60 ml / 2 fl oz / 4 tbsp extra-virgin olive oil
1 fresh sprig marjoram
1 fresh sprig sage
salt, to taste
black pepper, freshly ground
120 g / 4 fl oz / ½ US cup lentil stock, hot
    (left over from cooking the lentils)
5 g / 1 tsp (half a palmful) coarse sea salt
1½ tbsp acacia honey (substitute with agave or maple syrup
    for a vegan version)

How you make it

If using dry lentils, rinse them in cold running water. Put the lentils in a saucepan and cover with cold unsalted water. Add 1 onion, the clove of garlic and the bay leaf and bring to the boil on a medium heat. Boil for 2 to 3 minutes, reduce the heat and simmer for a further 15 to 20 minutes. Cooking time depends on the age of the lentils as older pulses lose their moisture and take longer to cook. 5 minutes before the end of cooking time, check the texture of the lentils. You want them tender but still retaining a firm texture. Do not overcook or they will become mushy.

Chop the other onion and set to one side in a small bowl. Wash the peppers, take the seeds out and cut them into thin slices.

Into a casserole, put the extra-virgin olive oil, the onion, the herbs, the salt and the ground pepper. Stirring occasionally, gently fry on a low heat. After 5 minutes, add the peppers, mixing in the *soffritto* (or aromatic flavour base). Add ½ US cup of the hot lentil stock and cook for a further 15 minutes until the juice has partially evaporated.

When the lentils are cooked, add half a palmful of sea salt and turn the heat off. Drain the boiled lentils, add to the peppers and cook for a further 5 minutes. Season with salt (to taste). Stir in the honey or syrup and cook for further a 5 minutes, mixing well to flavour.

Serve hot.

Versatility

The trick to preserving the 'goodness' of extra-virgin olive oil when making *soffritto*, or cooking with oil in general, is to cook it on a low heat. Experiment with using olive oil cold, too, perhaps drizzled over the cooked dish just before serving it.

Another tip is to mix the extra-virgin olive oil with water prior to or during cooking so that the onions soften and glaze, ensuring that the *soffritto* is still full of flavour while reducing the amount of fat used in the dish – even if it is 'healthy' fat!

Contorni

Zucchine Trifolate all'Italiana

Italian-style Sautéed Courgettes

Suitable for children and adults
Preparation time: 10 minutes
Cooking time: 20 minutes
Serves 4 people

What you need

5 medium courgettes / zucchini, sliced
1 large onion, peeled and finely sliced
1–2 cloves garlic (according to taste), peeled and crushed
60 ml / 2 fl oz / 4 tbsp extra-virgin olive oil
200 ml / 6¾ fl oz / ¾ US cup hot vegetable stock
1 sprig fresh oregano (or substitute with ½ tsp dry oregano)
½ bunch flat-leaf parsley, chopped
salt, to taste
black pepper, freshly ground

How you make it

Wash the courgettes / zucchini. Slice and set to one side.

Finely slice the onion. Crush the garlic.

Heat the oil in a large frying pan, add the onion and the garlic. Cook on a low heat until the onion has softened and starts turning brown.

Add the courgettes / zucchini and fry for about 5 minutes, stirring constantly. Add the hot vegetable stock, the oregano, half the parsley, salt and pepper and gently simmer for approximately 10 minutes until the liquid has almost evaporated.

Serve the courgettes / zucchini topped with a sprinkle of the remaining fresh parsley and freshly ground black pepper.

Terrina di Porri

Leek 'Hot Pot'

This dish is a beautiful side dish for both meat and fish. It can also be served as a starter on its own or as a main course with a salad for lunch or a light dinner. In my family, we all adore leeks and this is a very tasty way of enjoying them.

Suitable for children and adults
Preparation time: 15 minutes
Cooking time: 15 minutes
Serves 4 people

What you need
4 large leeks, trimmed and halved
30 ml / 1 fl oz / 2 tbsp extra-virgin olive oil
30 g / 1 oz / ¼ stick butter
150 g Fontina cheese, cubed (or substitute
    with Emmenthaler or Gruyère)
200 ml / 6¾ fl oz / ¾ US cup double / heavy cream
50 g / 1¾ oz / ½ US cup breadcrumbs, dry
salt
pepper

How you make it
Pre-heat the oven to 180°C / 350°F / Gas Mark 4.

Trim and wash the leeks. Cut them in half.

Into a grill pan, pour the olive oil, heat it and, when hot, put the leeks on to braise for 5 minutes, constantly turning them.

Grease 4 ovenproof moulds/bowls with butter.

Cut the cheese into very small cubes. Mix the leeks with the cream, the cheese, salt and pepper then fill the moulds/bowls with this mixture. Sprinkle a generous amount of breadcrumbs over the top of each.

Bake for 10 minutes until the breadcrumbs are golden and the cheese is melted.

Serve hot.

Fagiolini al Pomodoro e Cipolla

Green Beans in Tomato and Onion Sauce

Suitable for children and adults
Preparation time: 15 minutes
Cooking time: 25 minutes
Serves 4 people

What you need
450 g / 15 ¾ oz / 3 ½ US cups fresh green beans
1 large onion
4 ripe plum tomatoes (ripe medium vine tomatoes are
    a good substitute)
60 ml / 2 fl oz / 4 tbsp extra-virgin olive oil
250 ml / 8 ½ fl oz / 1 US cup vegetable stock
1 bay leaf
a pinch of salt
black pepper, ground

How you make it
Wash, top and tail the green beans.

Finely chop the onion. Wash and chop the tomatoes.

Put all the ingredients into a casserole.

Cook on a low heat for about 20 to 25 minutes, until the beans are tender.

Melodia di Carote, Cavolo Rosso e Verde e Spicchi di Arancia

Carrot, Cabbage and Orange Medley

Suitable for children and adults
Preparation time: 15 minutes
Serves 4 people

What you need

3 medium carrots, peeled and grated
¼ small red cabbage, thinly sliced
¼ small white cabbage, thinly sliced
1 orange, peeled
½ lemon, juice of
60 ml / 2 fl oz / 4 tbsp extra-virgin olive oil
a pinch of salt
a generous amount of balsamic vinegar glaze
    (or substitute with balsamic vinegar)
white pepper

How you make it

Peel and grate the carrots. Wash and thinly slice the cabbage. Peel the orange and separate into segments, removing the pith / albedo.

Squeeze out the lemon juice and beat into the olive oil, salt and pepper.

Put the ingredients into a large salad bowl. Mix them with the dressing and top with a generous amount of balsamic vinegar glaze.

Versatility

Add a handful of organic sultanas, 5 chopped and ready-to-eat organic apricots (if not already re-hydrated, soak them in a little warm water to plump them up) and 1 tablespoon of gomasio (a dry condiment made from toasted sesame seeds and salt) to create an even more interesting crossover of flavours.

Zucca e Finocchi Arrosto con Erbe

Roasted Pumpkin and Fennel with Herbs

Suitable for adults and adventurous children
Preparation time: 15 minutes
Cooking time: 40–50 minutes
Serves 4 people

What you need
1 small to medium pumpkin, cubed
3 fennel bulbs, quartered
90 ml / 3 fl oz / 6 tbsp extra-virgin olive oil
½ tsp dry fennel seeds
1 sprig fresh rosemary
1 sprig fresh sage
1 sprig fresh marjoram
1 sprig fresh thyme
½ tsp salt
a generous pinch of ground nutmeg (optional)

How you make it
Pre-heat the oven to 180°C / 350°F / Gas Mark 4.

Skin the pumpkin, remove the seeds and cut the flesh into big cubes.

Remove the outer leaves of the fennel (usually the first few are the harder ones). Quarter the fennel and cut the stems. Shred the herbs.

Into a large mixing bowl, pour the olive oil, add the fennel seeds and the herbs. Add the pumpkin and the fennel and stir well. Add a pinch of salt (to taste).

Put the dressed vegetables into a large, square oven tray and bake for 40 minutes until soft and golden. Stir the vegetables occasionally so that they cook evenly.

Versatility
Combine 2 tablespoons of extra-virgin olive oil, a knob of butter, a generous pinch of salt, a generous pinch of ground nutmeg and a generous pinch of sweet paprika, stirring well. If you like spicy food, add a generous pinch of dry chilly pepper and hot paprika. Pour the mixture in a frying pan and gently heat. Add 100 g / 3½ oz peeled hazelnuts or 100 g / 3½ oz peeled almonds, turn the heat to low / medium and, constantly stirring, toast the nuts until gold and coated. Stir the nuts into the roasted pumpkin and fennel. Once cooked, finely chop half a bunch of flat-leaf parsley and sprinkle over the top, mix well and serve.

Coste Saltate

Sautéed Swiss Chard

Suitable for children and adults
Preparation time: 20 minutes
Cooking time: 20 minutes
Serves 4 people

What you need

500 g / 17½ oz / 14 US cups Swiss chard, leaves
1 medium onion, peeled and finely sliced
1–2 cloves garlic (according to taste), peeled and crushed
60 ml / 2 fl oz / 4 tbsp extra-virgin olive oil
1 tbsp water

Optional:
Creole spice mix, freshly ground (or substitute with
    freshly ground white, black, green and pink peppercorns
    mixed together)

How you make it

Clean the Swiss chard and remove the bottom of each stem.
Cut the leaves, separating them from the stems, and wash
them in cold water.

Peel and finely slice the onion. Peel and crush the garlic.

Into a large frying pan (with a lid, used later), add 1
tablespoon of olive oil, 1 tablespoon of water, the onion and
the garlic and cook on a low heat, stirring and making sure
the garlic does not burn. Add the chards dripping with water.
Cover with a lid and cook for 20 minutes.

Once cooked, add the remaining olive oil.

Season with ground Creole spice mix, if desired.

Serve hot.

Versatility

To make this very easy recipe a little more elaborate and
presented, if you like, as a starter, make a béchamel sauce,
pour it over the Swiss chard in an ovenproof dish and bake for
20 minutes. Serve hot. You will find the recipe for béchamel
in the Lamb in yellow sauce recipe on page 216.

Insalata di Barbabietole, Caprino e Pinoli Tostati, Spolverata con Erba Cipollina e Pepe Rosa

Beetroot, Goat's Cheese and Toasted Pinenut Salad sprinkled with Zingy Chives and Pink Peppercorns

Suitable for adults and adventurous children
Preparation time: 15 minutes (plus 3 to 4 minutes
    for toasting the pine nuts)
Serves 4 people

What you need

½ bunch fresh chives
4 medium pre-cooked beetroots, cubed
150 g / 5¼ oz caprino (or substitute with any fresh,
    soft goat's cheese)
a pinch of salt
1 tsp cider vinegar
60 ml / 2 fl oz / 4 tbsp extra-virgin olive oil
100 g / 3½ oz / ¾ US cup pine nuts

Optional:
a few pink peppercorns, crushed
blueberry balsamic glaze (available from Italian delis)

How you make it

Wash and finely chop the chives and set to one side.

Cut the beetroots into small cubes.

In a large salad bowl, mix the salt, the cider vinegar and the extra-virgin olive oil. Add the beetroot cubes and mix well. Add the cheese and gently mix all together.

Heat a medium-sized frying pan. When hot, after about 2 minutes, put the pine nuts in to toast. Remove the pan from the heat. Stir constantly and quickly, making sure the pine nuts do not burn. If necessary, return the pan to the heat. When the pine nuts turn to a golden colour, after about 3 to 4 minutes, they are ready.

Add the pine nuts to the salad and top with chives to decorate.

Crush some pink peppercorns and sprinkle over the top, to taste. Squirt some fruity balsamic glaze, too, if desired – it will accentuate the sweet and sour flavours of this salad.

Versatility

This side dish can also be presented as a starter, served in individual bowls.

Cavolfiore Fritto

Fried Cauliflower Florets

Suitable for children and adults
Preparation time: 20 minutes
Cooking time: 20 minutes
Serves 4 people

What you need
1 large cauliflower, cut in florets
a pinch of salt
2 eggs
50 ml / 1¾ fl oz / ¼ US cup cold sparkling water / cold beer
   (if cooking for adults only)
60 g / 2 oz / ½ US cup white plain / all-purpose flour,
   plus some to coat the cauliflower
120 ml / 4 fl oz / 8 tbsp sunflower oil
coarse sea salt

How you make it
Wash and cut the cauliflower separating the florets from the stem.

To cook the cauliflower, bring a medium saucepan of water to the boil. Add a pinch of salt, the cauliflower and cook for 5 minutes. Drain and set to one side.

Prepare the batter by beating the eggs, stirring in the flour a little at the time and adding the water / beer plus a pinch of salt.

Heat the sunflower oil in a large frying pan. Dip the cauliflower in flour and then in the batter. When the oil is hot, fry the cauliflower until it turns a golden colour. Drain on kitchen paper.

Sprinkle with coarse sea salt and serve immediately.

Patate Cremose al Rosmarino

Creamy Potatoes with Rosemary

Suitable for children and adults
Preparation time: 15 minutes
Cooking time: 35 minutes
Serves 4–6 people

What you need
1 large onion, peeled and finely chopped
4 large potatoes, peeled and diced
200 g / 7 oz / 1¾ sticks butter
400 ml / 13½ fl oz / 1¾ US cups milk, hot
30 g / 1 oz / ¼ US cup white plain / all-purpose flour
a generous pinch of ground nutmeg
1 tsp coarse sea salt
1 bunch fresh rosemary
100 ml / 3⅓ fl oz / ⅓ US cup water, hot
black pepper, freshly ground

How you make it
Peel and finely chop the onions and set to one side. Peel and dice the potatoes and set to one side.

In a frying pan, melt 50 g / 1¾ oz of butter on a low heat. Add the onion and cook until soft.

Heat the milk, making sure that it does not boil.

In a casserole (with a lid, and preferably one made of clay if you have one), melt the rest of the butter on a low heat. Add the flour a little bit at a time, stirring constantly. Add the nutmeg, the salt, the onions, the rosemary, the potatoes and stir well. Cook for 2 or 3 minutes.

Add the hot milk and the hot water. Cover with a lid and cook, stirring occasionally, on a low heat for 30 minutes or until the liquid has turned creamy and the potatoes are soft. Season with black pepper, to taste, and serve.

Spinaci Saltati All'aglio con Taleggio e Noci

Sautéed Spinach in Garlic with Taleggio and Walnuts

Suitable for adults and adventurous children
Preparation time: 15 minutes
Cooking time: 10–15 minutes
Serves 4 people

What you need
500 g / 17½ oz / 16¾ US cups fresh spinach
160 g / 6 oz Taleggio cheese, diced (or substitute
    with Fontina, Bel Paese or Gouda)
30 ml / 1 fl oz / 2 tbsp extra-virgin olive oil
3 cloves garlic, peeled and sliced
60 g / 2 oz / ½ US cup walnut pieces (kernels)
salt
a generous pinch of ground nutmeg

How you make it
Wash and pat dry the spinach. Peel and finely chop
the garlic.

Dice the cheese and set to one side.

Into a large frying pan (with a lid, used later), pour the olive
oil and add the garlic. Lightly fry on a low heat, making sure
the garlic does not burn.

Add the spinach, cover with a lid and cook for about 7 to 10
minutes (according to whether you like spinach just tender or
well cooked), until the spinach wilts. Add the walnuts and stir.
Season with salt, to taste, and the nutmeg. Add the cheese at
the last minute of cooking.

Mix all the ingredients together and serve immediately.

Insalata Romana Fresca e Croccante con Fave e Pecorino

Crunchy Lettuce and Broad Bean Salad with Pecorino Cheese

Suitable for children and adults
Preparation time: 15 minutes
Serves 4 people

What you need
1 romaine / cos lettuce
1 litre / 34 fl oz / 4¼ US cups water
a pinch of salt
150 g / 5¼ oz / 1¼ US cups fresh broad beans /
    fava beans, podded
½ lemon, juice of
150 g / 5¼ oz medium-matured pecorino, shavings
75 ml / 2½ fl oz / 5 tbsp extra-virgin olive oil
4 sprigs fresh mint, torn
½ tsp crushed pink peppercorns
freshly ground black pepper

How you make it
Wash, pat dry and slice the lettuce, then set to one side.

Bring the water to the boil in a large saucepan.

When the water reaches boiling point, add the salt and the broad beans and cook for 2 to 3 minutes. Once cooked, drain, run under cold water and set to one side.

Squeeze the ½ lemon for its juice. Prepare the dressing by mixing a little salt, pepper, the lemon juice, the olive oil and the mint together. Lightly beat the ingredients to mix and fully release the dressing's flavours.

In a bowl, gently stir in the lettuce leaves, the broad beans and the dressing. Shave the pecorino cheese over the top and sprinkle with the crushed pink peppercorns.

This dish can be served in one large bowl or in individual serving bowls.

Piselli, Prosciutto e Cipollotti

Peas, Ham and Spring Onions

Suitable for children and adults
Preparation time: 10 minutes
Cooking time: 10 minutes
Serves 4 people

What you need

1 bunch continental salad onions, chopped
100 g / 4 oz / 1 thick slice *prosciutto cotto*, diced
 (or substitute with gammon)
60 ml / 2 fl oz / 4 tbsp extra-virgin olive oil
200 g / 7 oz / 1¼ US cups peas
salt
black pepper, freshly ground

How you make it

Top and tail the salad onions. Wash and chop them.

Dice the ham.

Into a frying pan, put the olive oil and the onions on a low
heat and cook for 3 minutes.

Add the prosciutto and cook until the onions are soft.

Add salt.

Add the peas and cook for a further 3 minutes.

Serve hot.

Versatility

If you like a smoky flavour, use *Prosciutto di Praga* (smoked
roast ham), available from Italian delis or good quality
supermarkets.

This much-loved side dish can also be used as a topping
for pasta. Use penne if you fancy a primo with these
ingredients, which combine the delicate flavour of the peas
and the spring onions with the consistency and fullness of
the prosciutto.

Dolci

Tortionata all'Andreina

Andreina's Tortionata

Tortionata or *sbrisolona* has always been one of my favourites, but I have never been quite sure which would be the 'perfect' way to make it. One day, when chef Tito Bergamaschi and I were reminiscing about our childhoods, we recalled tortionata, and Tito said that his mother might just have had the 'perfect' recipe. I was delighted, therefore, when Andreina kindly passed her recipe on to me.

Tortionata is best enjoyed either as an after-dinner cake, accompanied by a sweet dessert wine, or broken into crumbly pieces and dunked in the breakfast milk! The cake is very popular in the Lombardy and Veneto regions of Italy. In Venetian dialect, it is called *sbrisolona*, which literally means 'something that crumbles'. In Lombardy, it is commonly served with icing sugar (confectioner's sugar), while in Veneto the icing sugar is optional. Enjoy choosing which regional tradition to follow!

Suitable for children and adults
Preparation time: 15 minutes
Cooking time: 1 hour
Serves 4–6 people

What you need
220 g / 7¾ oz / 1¾ US cups white plain / all-purpose flour
100 g / 3½ oz / ½ US cup caster / superfine sugar
100 g / 3½ oz / peeled almonds, chopped
185 g / 6½ oz / 1⅗ sticks unsalted butter
a pinch of salt
icing / confectioner's sugar to decorate, if desired

How you make it
Pre-heat the oven to 150°C / 300°F / Gas Mark 2.

Sift the flour into a large metal mixing bowl.

Add all the ingredients, except the icing / confectioner's sugar, and mix thoroughly.

Grease and flour a 2-cm (¾ in) high × 20-cm (8 in) diameter cake tin (or use a shaped one if you wish). Line the tin with baking paper / parchment.

Transfer the mix into the cake tin, pressing it with a fork to spread it evenly.

Bake for 1 hour until golden. Let the cake cool down before serving it.

Sprinkle with icing / confectioner's sugar, if you wish.

Versatility
Andreina would serve her tortionata sprinkled with icing / confectioner's sugar on top and broken into pieces. As you can see in the photograph, I have given you my 'love heart' version, which can be made either for a specific romantic occasion or just as a little sign of affection for your family and friends.

Duetto di Pesche
Peach Duet

A very simple and quick recipe that allows you to indulge in three very Italian delicacies: peaches, lemons and red wine. Children and adults together enjoy the peaches with a syrup sauce made of lemon, for the little ones, and wine for the adults.

In the summer, my grandfather used to finish his meal with the latter when there was no other dessert. He also used to make *Pesche al limone* for me when I was a child and, with time, I started to taste one or two peaches in red wine… it is still hard to tell which is my favourite!

Enjoy the recipes as they are, or accompanied with vanilla or cinnamon ice cream.

Pesche al Limone
Peaches in Lemon Syrup

Suitable for children and adults
Preparation time: 10 minutes
Marinating / chilling time: 30 minutes
Serves 4 people

What you need
2 glasses warm water
60 g / 2 oz / ⅓ US cup demerara / raw sugar
2 lemons, juice of
1 sprig fresh mint
4 medium–large peaches / 8 small peaches

How you make it
Into a bowl, pour 2 glasses of warm water. Add and dissolve the sugar. Add the juice of the 2 lemons, a sprig of mint and stir well.

Slice each peach and place into individual bowls. Top up with the syrup and add a sprig of mint as a garnish.

Chill in the fridge for 30 minutes and then serve with vanilla or cinnamon ice cream, if desired.

Pesche al Vino Rosso
Peaches in Red Wine

Suitable for adults only
Preparation time: 10 minutes
Marinating / chilling time: 30 minutes
Serves 4 people

What you need
2 glasses of Italian red wine
30 g / 1 oz / ⅛ US cup demerara / raw sugar
4 medium–large peaches / 8 small peaches
4 cloves

How you make it
Set out four glasses and pour ½ a glass of red wine into each. Divide the sugar between the four glasses, allowing it to dissolve in the wine.

Place 1 clove into each glass of wine.

Slice the peaches and put them in the wine, shared across the four glasses.

Put in the fridge to marinate for 30 minutes. Serve with a scoop of vanilla ice cream on top, if desired.

Salame di Cioccolato

Chocolate Salami

This is an old-fashioned, much-loved, traditional and comforting cake. My friend Catriona and her two children, who tried out the recipe for me before the book was published, described it as 'easy peasy and totally scrummy!'... see if you share their views?

It is generally advised that pregnant women, babies and toddlers avoid eating products that contain raw eggs, so use pasteurised eggs if making *Salame di Cioccolato* for them.

Suitable for adults and children above 5 years old
Preparation time: 20 minutes
Setting time: 2 hours in the fridge (minimum)
Serves 4 people

What you need
200 g / 7 oz plain biscuits / cookies
2 egg yolks
60 g / 2⅛ oz / ⅓ US cup brown sugar
50 g / 1¾ oz / ½ stick butter, melted
25 g / ⅞ oz / 14 tsp bitter cocoa powder

How you make it
Crumble the biscuits and set to one side.

Beat the egg yolks with half of the sugar until you obtain a creamy mixture of a pale yellow colour. Melt the butter and add to the eggs. Add the rest of the sugar, the cocoa powder and stir well.

Add the biscuits to the mixture and stir well.

Using your hands, roll the mixture out in a long shape, similar to salami, of approximately 6 to 7 cm (2½ to 2¾ in) in diameter.

Wrap it in cling film. Put it in the fridge to set for 2 to 3 hours.

Take the chocolate *salame* out of the fridge. Slice it and serve.

Torta di Ricotta

Italian Cheesecake

Suitable for children and adults
Preparation time: 40 minutes (plus resting time)
Cooking time: 50 minutes
Serves 6–8 people

What you need

For the pastry:
350 g / 12½ oz / 2½ US cups white plain / all-purpose flour,
    plus extra for dusting
½ tsp salt
20 g / ¾ oz / 1½ tbsp granulated / white sugar
250 g / 8¾ oz / 2½ sticks butter – diced into very small
    pieces (kept cold), plus extra for greasing
75 ml / 2½ fl oz / ⅓ US cup ice-cold water

For the filling:
60 ml / 2 fl oz / ¼ US cup warm water (or half warm water
    and half rum)
40 g / 4 tbsp sultanas / raisins
2 egg yolks
100 g / 3½ oz / ½ US cup caster /superfine sugar
1 tbsp vanilla extract
½ tsp ground cinnamon
¼ tsp ground nutmeg
10 g / 1 tbsp candied orange peel
¼ lemon, grated peel / zest of
300 g / 10½ oz ricotta
4 egg whites

Optional:
20 g / 1½ tbsp chocolate chips

How you make it

For the pastry:
Half an hour before starting to make the torta, put the mixing bowl / food processor equipment and all the kitchen tools you will be using into the freezer. Cold equipment will help with the pastry-making process as one of the tricks for successfully making pastry is to keep it cool while working with it. If you wish to work the dough by hand using the rub-in method, sieve the flour to form a mound on a cold surface, such as marble or glass. Otherwise, use a large glass or steel mixing bowl. Add the salt and the sugar. Run your hands under cold water and quickly pat dry. Make a hole into the mound and add the cold cubed butter, working the ingredients using the tips of your fingers to form crumbs. Then, add one spoonful of cold water at a time, working the dough quickly until a sticky mass is formed. Avoid overworking or overheating the dough.

If you prefer, put the flour, the cold cubed butter, the sugar, the salt and the lemon zest in a food processor, whizz it on a medium/high setting for 1 minute to blend the ingredients, until a 'sandy', crumbly mixture is formed. Add water one tablespoon at a time, gently stirring with the help of a fork until the dough sticks together. This method keeps the dough cool and malleable.

Run your hands under cold water and quickly pat dry. Remove the dough from the food processor, if you are using one.

Shape the dough into a ball, flatten it into a disc, wrap it in cling film / plastic wrap and put it in the fridge to rest for 1 hour.

In the meantime, prepare the filling.

For the filling:
Soak the sultanas / raisins in the warm water (and rum, if used).

Separate the eggs. Using an electric hand-held whisk, beat the 2 egg yolks and the sugar until the mixture becomes a pale yellow colour. Add the vanilla extract, the cinnamon, the nutmeg, the orange peel and the lemon zest and gently mix for a few minutes until the mixture is smooth.

Fold the cheese into the egg yolk mixture, one spoonful at a time, and mix.

In a separate bowl, and with a clean and dry whisk, beat the 4 egg whites until they form stiff peaks. Gently fold the egg whites into the mixture one spoonful at a time. You will smell a beautiful aroma of spices and fresh lemon emanating from the mixture.

Squeeze the water (and rum, if used) out of the sultanas / raisins and stir them into the mixture.

Stir in the chocolate chips to the mixture if you are using them.

Keep the mixture to one side.

For the Italian cheesecake:
Pre-heat the oven to 180°C / 350°F / Gas Mark 4.

Butter and flour a 24-cm (9-½ in) round oven / tart tin, preferably one with a removable base.

Take half of the pastry out of the fridge. Using a rolling pin, roll the pastry out on a floured surface. Lay the pastry onto the oven tin to make the base of the cake. Using the prongs of a fork, make a few holes scattered around the pastry. Put the pastry in the freezer to rest for 30 minutes.

Roll the remaining pastry out and, using a pastry cutter or a knife, cut flat strips of pastry of about 1½ cm / ¾ in and put to one side, on a plate, in the fridge.

Take the base of the cake out of the freezer and bake it 'blind' using baking / parchment paper and 'baking beans' for 15 minutes until it dries up a little. Remove the paper and the baking beans, then continue to bake for another 15 to 20 minutes until the colour turns light gold. Take it out of the oven and leave it to rest for 5 minutes. Meanwhile, take the pastry strips out of the fridge.

Pour the ricotta mixture onto the pastry base. Place the strips of pastry crossways on top of the mixture.

Re-bake the cake for 25 to 30 minutes until the pastry is gold and the ricotta mixture has set. Check occasionally that the ricotta mixture does not turn brown – if the colour of the ricotta starts to darken, cover with aluminium / kitchen foil to avoid it burning. Ovens vary, so keep an eye on your pastry and ensure that it dries out when you first bake it without the filling, ready to be filled, otherwise the base does not cook properly. Equally, ensure that, when the cake is at the last stage of baking, the pastry cooks, but the filling does not burn.

Leave the cake to cool down before serving.

Tiramisù Unico

The One and Only Tiramisu

Tiramisu is one of the classics among Italian desserts. It is traditionally prepared using coffee, but, for younger children or anyone who does not tolerate coffee, you can substitute coffee with cold milk or with the caffeine-free alternative *caffè d'orzo*. Orzo is the Italian barley from which the beverage is made; other, branded names for similar roasted grain, caffeine-free beverages include barleycup, in the UK, caro elsewhere in Europe and pero in the USA.

There are two ways to make the cream for the tiramisu: one is with raw eggs, as featured in the recipe below; the other uses the *bagno maria* (bain-marie) method, featured in the Versatility section. Young children and pregnant women are both advised to avoid consuming raw eggs and so should only be served tiramisu made using the *bagno maria* method and pasteurised eggs.

Suitable for children and adults
Preparation time: 30 minutes
Chilling time: 3 hours in the fridge (minimum)
Serves 10–12 people

What you need
6 eggs
100 g / 3½ oz / scant ½ US cup granulated / white sugar
600 g / 21⅓ oz mascarpone cheese
350 ml / 11¾ fl oz / 1½ US cups strong filter coffee
300 g / 10½ oz *savoiardi* / ladyfinger biscuits
    (or substitute with sponge fingers)
50 g / 1¾ oz / heaped ⅓ US cups 70% bittersweet cocoa powder
    or 150 g / 5 oz / 1½ US cups 70% cocoa solids / bittersweet chocolate, shavings

Optional (suitable for adults):
3 cl (30 ml) / 1 fl oz Marsala all'uovo wine (or substitute with an Italian sweet dessert wine of your choice)

How you make it
Between two medium-sized mixing bowls, separate the egg yolks from the egg whites.

Add 6 tablespoons of sugar to the 6 yolks and beat with an electric whisk on a high setting until the mixture is soft and of a pale yellow colour.

Wash and dry the electric whisk before beating the egg whites (next step), as any yolk or water will prevent the egg whites from firming. Now, using the electric whisk, beat the egg whites until they form stiff peaks.

Transfer the yolk cream into a large mixing bowl, fold in the mascarpone, one spoonful at a time, stirring gently with a hand whisk. Do not over-stir the mascarpone. Using a stainless steel spoon, fold in the egg whites one spoonful at a time, stirring gently with a hand whisk.

Pour the coffee into a large bowl and allow to cool to room temperature. Then dip one *savoiardo* in at a time and arrange a layer of biscuits in a deep, medium-sized, ceramic or glass container suitable for the fridge. You may not use the full quantity of the coffee, or you might need to add another 2 to 3 shots of coffee; it depends on the thickness of the biscuits and how much liquid they absorb. They should be moist, but not soggy.

Spoon and layer on some of the mascarpone mixture and then continue to layer, alternating the ingredients. The final, top layer should be made of the mascarpone mixture. The more layers, the softer, creamier and moist your tiramisu will be.

Chill in the fridge for a minimum of 3 hours to set. Tiramisu can be prepared a day in advance and left to chill, moisten and fully flavour in the fridge.

Once the tiramisu has chilled in the fridge, and just before serving, dust with dark chocolate cocoa powder or shave some dark chocolate over the top, depending on if you like a full smooth or crunchy texture. If you make your tiramisu a day in advance, though, sprinkle the cocoa powder or the chocolate shavings just before serving it.

Optional (for adults):
Add 30 cl (300 ml) / 10 fl oz Marsala all'uovo wine or any sweet Italian dessert wine (such as Vin Santo or Passito) to the coffee to moisten the *savoiardi* biscuits in.

For a fruity version of tiramisu:
'Fruity tiramisu' can be made by using either 350 ml of cold milk or pressed apple juice to moisten the *savoiardi* biscuits. Simply dip one *savoiardo* biscuit at a time into the juice / milk and arrange on the bottom of the container to form the first layer of your fruity tiramisu. Spoon and spread a layer of mascarpone cream onto the first layer of *savoiardi* biscuits. Thinly slice ripe fruit of your choice from strawberries, raspberries, apricots, peaches (skin removed) or kiwi. Add a layer of sliced fruit to the layers in the container. Continue layering, alternating the ingredients and making sure the top layer comprises the mascarpone cream, if using peaches or apricots; if using strawberries, raspberries and kiwi, lay them on the top layer. Raspberries can be left whole; strawberries can be halved or sliced; kiwi should be sliced. Dust with icing / confectioner's sugar as a topping and chill in the fridge for 3 hours minimum. For the adult version, mix 10 cl (100 ml) / 3 ½ fl oz of sweet wine with 250 ml / 8⅓ fl oz / 1 US cup of pressed apple juice, and dip the *savoiardi* biscuits in.

Versatility
If you do not wish to make tiramisu using raw eggs, the recipe could incorporate a modern version of *zabaione* instead. In a glass bowl, lightly beat the egg yolks (only). Combine them with the sugar and, using an electric whisk, whisk the two ingredients until a smooth pale colour and creamy mixture is obtained (up to 10 minutes). Put a medium-sized saucepan filled half way with water onto a medium heat and bring to the boil. When the water reaches boiling point, turn the heat down, place the glass bowl containing the egg mixture onto the saucepan and gently stir until it thickens into a smooth cream. Do not boil. Let the *zabaione* cool down, then incorporate the mascarpone cheese as per the recipe above. From this point, you can follow the method above to complete your tiramisu.

Torta di Mele della Zia

Auntie's Apple Cake

I can't take any credit for this recipe, which is the result of my mother's cooking heritage passed on to my sister and her own great culinary skills. You might have gathered by now that at home, generation after generation, we all loved, and still love, food, cooking and hosting. My girls have many times been spoiled with this cake by their auntie. They can be sure that it will be one of those thick, crusty on the outside, fluffy light and moist on the inside cakes that make your mouth water just at the thought of it!

Zia ('auntie' in Italian), like the majority of Italian ladies, eats her fair share, too, but has a very slender figure, mainly due to a good Mediterranean diet, and also because she puts no butter in this cake. No wonder it appeals to both children and adults!

Suitable for children and adults
Preparation time: 20 minutes
Cooking time: 50 minutes
Serves 6 people

What you need

22 g / ¾ oz sultanas / raisins, soaked in water and vanilla extract (for children) or rum (for adults)
5 apples (Renetta / Golden Reinette variety, if available), peeled and thinly sliced
2 eggs, at room temperature
200 g / 7 oz / 1 US cup demerara / raw sugar
150 ml / 5 fl oz / ¾ US cup sunflower oil
70 ml / 2¼ fl oz / ¼ US cup milk, at room temperature
350 g / 12 oz / 2¾ US cups plain white / all-purpose flour
1 tsp ground cinnamon
16 g / ½ oz / 4½ US tsp baking powder

How you make it

Pre-heat the oven to 180°C / 350°F / Gas Mark 4.

Soak the sultanas to soften, either in water and vanilla extract or in rum, depending on if you are making the cake for both children and adults or for adults only.

Peel and thinly slice the apples and put to one side.

In a large mixing bowl, whisk the eggs and the sugar. Add the sunflower oil, the milk and stir well. Sift the flour and add to the mixture, stirring well. Drain the sultanas, squeeze the liquid out and put to one side.

Add the cinnamon, the sultanas, the sliced apples and stir well. Add the baking powder at the end, making sure the mixture is smooth.

Pour the mixture into a spring / spring form cake tin. Bake for 50 minutes.

Allow the cake to cool before serving it.

Optional:
Dust with icing / confectioner's sugar to decorate.

Versatility

I have made this cake using spelt flour instead of wheat flour and my girls loved it. By substituting the flour in this way, the cake can also be enjoyed by people suffering from wheat intolerance – and without compromising on the flavour.

Crostata di Frutta

Fruit Tart

Suitable for children and adults
Preparation time: 40 minutes
Cooking time: 40 minutes
Serves 4–6 people

What you need

For the pastry:
200 g / 7 oz / 1¾ sticks butter, cold and cut into small cubes
1 lemon, grated peel of
300 g / 10½ oz / 2⅖ cups white plain / all-purpose flour,
    plus extra for dusting
150 g / 5¼ oz / ⅗ US cup caster / superfine sugar
1 egg
1 egg yolk

For the filling:
a pinch of salt
fruit of your choice (e.g. mixed berries, peaches, apricots,
    plums, kiwi, tangerines, bananas, etc.)
2 tbsp apricot jam
4–5 tbsp hot water

How you make it

Pre-heat the oven to 170°C / 325°F / Gas Mark 3.

Cut the cold butter into small cubes and set to one side. Grate the lemon peel and set to one side. Sift the flour and add the sugar, the butter, the whole egg and the egg yolk, a pinch of salt and the grated lemon peel.

Run your hands under cold water. Pat dry.

Work the ingredients quickly into a pastry. Shape the pastry into a ball then wrap it in cling film and put it in the fridge to rest for 30 minutes.

Using a rolling pin, roll the pastry out.

Butter and flour a round pastry tin. Lay the pastry in the tin and prick with a fork in various places. Lay some greaseproof / wax paper or aluminium / kitchen foil on top of the pastry. Cover with some dry beans ('baking beans') on top.

Bake for 40 minutes at 170°C / 325°F / Gas Mark 3. When cooked, remove the beans and let it cool down.

Meanwhile, peel and slice the fruit. You can decide to have a mixed fruit tart, a mixed berries tart or focus on a single type of fruit. The classic Italian recipe uses mixed fruit.

Dilute the tablespoon of jam with 4 to 5 tablespoons of hot water, depending on the consistency of the jam. The more liquid the jam, the less water you'll need. Spread half of the diluted jam onto the pastry and keep the rest to one side. Use your judgement regarding whether to dilute more or fewer tablespoons of jam with water.

Lay the fruit in a concentric circle. Once the jam / water jelly is at room temperature, spread it on top of the fruit.

Put the tart in the fridge for 30 to 45 minutes.

Mele al Cartoccio

Apple Parcel

Suitable for children and adults
Preparation time: 30 minutes (plus resting
    time for the pastry)
Cooking time: 45–50 minutes
Serves 4–6 people

What you need
For the pastry:
250 g / 8¾ oz / 2 US cups white plain / all-purpose flour,
    plus extra for dusting
a pinch of salt
125 g / 4⅖ oz / 1 stick butter (keep it cold), diced;
    plus extra for greasing and brushing
1 egg yolk
2 tsp cold water
icing / confectioner's sugar, to dust

For the filling:
100 g / 3½ oz sultanas
2 tbsp warm water
2 tbsp vanilla essence
1 kg / 2¼ lb golden apples
50 g / 1¾ oz / ¼ US cup demerara / raw sugar
1 tsp cinnamon
½ tsp nutmeg
½ fresh lemon, grated peel of
5 tbsp apricot jam
11¾ g / ½ oz ground almonds

How you make it
Pre-heat the oven to 180°C / 350°F / Gas Mark 4.

Soak the sultanas in water and vanilla essence.

Peel and finely slice the apples. Put the apples in a mixing
bowl adding the sugar, cinnamon, nutmeg, grated lemon
peel and apricot jam and stir well.

Squeeze the liquid out of the sultanas and add to the mixture,
mixing well. Leave the mixture to flavour whilst you are
preparing the pastry.

Into a large mixing bowl, sift the flour mixed with the salt and
the sugar . Cut the cold butter into small cubes.

Run your hands under cold water and pat dry. Quickly mix
the butter with the flour using your fingertips until a crumbly
consistency is obtained.

In a cup, beat the egg yolk and 1 teaspoon of cold water.
Pour it onto the mixture. Pour another teaspoon of cold water
onto the remaining egg yolk and pour into the mixture.

Quickly and lightly work the mixture into dough with your
fingertips. Do not overwork. Shape it into a ball. Wrap it in
cling film / plastic wrap and keep it in the fridge to rest for 1
hour before rolling it out.

Using a rolling pin, roll the pastry out on a floured surface into a rectangular sheet. Make sure the pastry is rolled as thin as possible. Sprinkle with the almonds. Fill the sheet of pastry with the apple mixture. Fold over, making sure the edges are well sealed.

Melt a knob of butter and brush onto the parcel.

Line a rectangular oven tray with buttered baking / parchment paper and place the parcel into the tray. If you do not have baking / parchment paper, grease the oven tray with butter and flour it.

Bake in the oven until the pastry has turned a golden colour (approximately 45 to 50 minutes).

Let the apple parcel cool down.

Dust with icing / confectioner's sugar and serve.

Crema del Pasticcere

Patissier Cream

This cream is incredibly versatile. It can be eaten on its own as an afternoon snack, as a dessert after dinner or used to fill cakes. It can be served warm or chilled.

In the Versatility section, you will find all the different ways of serving it.

Suitable for children and adults
Preparation time: 5 minutes
Cooking time: 10 minutes

What you need
5 egg yolks
100 g / 3½ oz / ½ US cup granulated / white sugar
½ litre / 17 fl oz / 2 US cups whole (full-cream) milk
50 g / 1¾ oz / ⅓ US cup potato flour
1 vanilla pod (bean)
¼ lemon, zest / grated peel of

How you make it
Keep a glass of milk out of the ½ litre to one side.

On a low heat, warm the rest of the milk with the vanilla pod and the lemon peel / zest. When warm, turn off and leave the milk to one side to flavour.

In a mixing bowl, beat the egg yolks and the sugar. Gently add the potato flour, by sifting it in, constantly stirring. Add the glass of milk a little at a time and mix well until forming a smooth cream.

Take the vanilla pod and the lemon peel out of the milk. Slowly add the milk to the cream, stirring constantly to obtain a smooth liquid mixture.

Transfer to a saucepan and gently heat for a few minutes, constantly stirring until the liquid mixture finally sets into a cream.

Versatility
If you wish to eat this warm, simply sprinkle some cocoa powder and enjoy! Alternatively, leave it to cool and then chill it in the fridge for a further 2 hours. Serve in single bowls with crushed amaretti (almond-flavoured) biscuits sprinkled over the top and / or 2 chocolate or almond thins as an accompaniment. Or, serve in single bowls with fresh sliced fruit, adding a shot of Maraschino cherry liquor for the adults.

Cioccolata Calda Densa

Very Thick Hot Chocolate

This afternoon treat is so popular in Milan that people actually arrange to meet specifically for a *cioccolata*, especially on wintery Sunday afternoons. Such meetings can be at home, using the recipe below, or in one of the many *bar pasticcerie* where high-quality handmade chocolate is served.

Suitable for children and adults
Preparation time: 5 minutes
Cooking time: 10 minutes
Serves 4–6 people

What you need
700 g / 23 fl oz / scant 3 US cups whole (full-cream) milk
100 g / 3½ oz / 1 US cup unsweetened dark / bittersweet cocoa powder (70% cocoa solids)
80 g / 2⅘ oz / ⅔ US cup granulated / white sugar
10 g / ¼ oz / 2 tsp potato flour or cornflour / cornstarch

How you make it
Pour the milk into a saucepan. Warm it on a low heat, without boiling it.

In a separate, medium-sized saucepan, mix the chocolate powder with the sugar. Turn the heat on low. Put the pan on the heat then gently and slowly pour the milk, a little at a time, stirring constantly. Once you have poured in all the milk and obtained a smooth mixture, combine the potato flour or cornflour (cornstarch) using a sieve and quickly and constantly stirring. Make sure no lumps are formed. Keep stirring for about 3 to 5 further minutes until the mixture thickens.

Serve hot as it is or add fresh whipped cream on top and sprinkle with cinnamon.

Versatility
I like to taste the bitterness of the dark chocolate, but, if you have a sweet tooth, add half a teaspoon of sugar to each cup and stir before serving.

Bicerin

Hot Chocolate Espresso

In Turin, the quality of chocolate production is excellent and here one can enjoy the traditional *bicerin*: a grown-up, 'twisted' version of hot chocolate mixed with espresso coffee. *Bicerin* in Piedmontese dialect means 'little glass', indicating the little glass in which this recipe is served. For a very special adult's treat, pour a little shot of your favourite brandy into your *bicerin*!

Suitable for adults only
Preparation time: 10 minutes
Cooking time: 10 minutes
Serves 8 people

What you need
700 ml / 23 ½ fl oz / 3 US cups whole (full-cream) milk
100 g / 3 ½ oz / 1 US cup dark bittersweet chocolate powder (70% cocoa solids)
80 g / 2 ⅘ oz / ⅔ US cup granulated / white sugar
10 g / ¼ oz / 2 tsp *maizena* (cornflour / cornstarch) or potato flour
8 cups / shots freshly made sugared espresso
fresh whipping cream / double (heavy) cream or freshly whipped cream, as a topping
a shot of brandy (depending on the occasion!)

How you make it
Pour the milk into a saucepan and warm on a low heat, without boiling it.

In another, medium-sized saucepan, mix the chocolate powder with the sugar and place on a low heat. Slowly add the warm milk, a little at a time, stirring constantly.

Once you have added all of the milk and obtained a smooth mixture, gradually incorporate the flour, using a sieve, and stirring constantly. Make sure no lumps are formed. Keep stirring for 3 to 5 further minutes, or until the mixture thickens.

Make the espresso coffee and share it out across 8 heat-resistant medium-sized glasses, filling each a third of the way to the top. Fill another third of each glass with the hot chocolate. Top up the remaining third of the glasses with fresh whipping cream / double (heavy) cream or freshly whipped cream (*see* Versatility tip below), as you wish. If you are adding brandy to your *bicerin*, either mix two-thirds of coffee to one-third of brandy or go half and half, depending on your taste.

Versatility
If you wish to include freshly whipped cream, you will need to start the recipe above by first whipping the cream (as follows) and storing it in the fridge for a few minutes. To make it, buy a tub of fresh whipping cream / double (heavy) cream and put it in the fridge. Place the large bowl, too, in which you will be whipping the cream into the fridge for 15 minutes. Pour the cooled cream in the bowl and whisk it using a hand-held electric whisk. The colder the cream and the bowl, the better the result. My mother always insisted on whipping the cream outside on the kitchen terrace with her coat on! She used to say that it was quicker and the cream turned out fluffier. I leave it to you, however, to decide whether or not to experiment with the 'out-in-the-cold whipping cream method'!

Cantucci

Cantucci Biscuits

These crunchy Tuscan *biscotti* (biscuits) are adored by children for dunking into milk and by adults for dipping into a Tuscan dessert wine called 'vin santo'. I learned how to make them from my friend Camilla as part of preparations for an annual festival held in the eco-village in which my family and I lived during the writing of this book. It was a moment of revelation! I was in Tuscany, making Tuscan *cantucci* guided by a Tuscan lady for a festival that sees an ancient Etruscan hamlet open up to the world in celebration of children, life, organic food, music and generosity of spirit.

The dough is very sticky so it is better to work it in small quantities. If you want to make more biscuits, repeat the recipe twice using the same measures. The day I made *cantucci* with Camilla, we made many kilos at a time, four hands and four arms working the sticky dough together on a very large marble surface – and our strength quickly sapping.

As a variation, you may wish to add dark chocolate shavings (70% cocoa solids) to your *cantucci*. I suggest you make two batches, one with chocolate and one without, as the two flavours complement each other and make the biscuits even more tempting!

Suitable for children and adults
Preparation time: 20 minutes
Cooking time: 20 minutes

What you need

3 eggs
250 g / 9 oz / 1¾ US cups white plain / all-purpose flour, plus extra for dusting
250 g / 8 oz / 1 US cup golden caster / superfine sugar
1 teaspoon set / whipped / creamed honey
20 g / ¾ oz / ⅛ US cup sultanas / raisins
50 g / 1¾ oz / ⅓ US cup almonds, peeled
¼ lemon, grated rind of (if making chocolate cantucci, do not add lemon rind)
4 g / ⅓ oz / 1 US tsp baking powder for cakes

Optional:
25 g / ¼ oz / 1 oz dark / bittersweet chocolate (70% cocoa solids), shavings

How you make it

Pre-heat the oven to 170°C (160°C if using a fan oven) / 325°F / Gas Mark 3.

Cut some non-stick baking / parchment paper to the size of the oven trays you will be using.

Using a small bowl, lightly beat 1 egg and keep to one side (for brushing the dough before baking it).

Sift the flour onto a flat surface, forming a mound. Add the sugar, keeping the shape of a mound. Make a well in the middle and break the 2 remaining eggs into it. Add the honey. Then, add the sultanas / raisins, almonds and the lemon rind / zest. (If you are making the cantucci with chocolate, do not add the lemon peel. Instead, using a sharp knife, shave the piece of chocolate into flakes and add to the dough.)

Add the baking powder.

Mix the ingredients together very quickly as the dough will become very sticky.

Dust a little flour on the surface. Be sparing with the flour, though, as too much will make the biscuits dry when cooked. Take some dough and roll it with your hands, applying very little pressure until a sausage of 2 cm to 3 cm (¾ in to 1¼ in) in diameter is formed. Gently place the sausage on a baking tray and brush with the beaten egg you have kept aside.

Roll out another sausage, brush it with egg and place it next to the first sausage you made, leaving a gap big enough to allow the dough to rise. Prepare the third sausage, place on the baking tray and bake the first batch for 20 minutes until the dough turns a golden colour. The perfect cantucci are crusty on the outside but a little chewy on the inside.

Repeat and bake the remaining dough sausages.

As soon as you take the dough sausages out of the oven, cut them diagonally into approximately 1½ cm (¾ in) thick slices. The cantucci will feel still a bit sticky; don't worry, they will dry out on the cooling rack.

Your cantucci are made! Let the biscuits cool down until they harden before serving.

Versatility

For the adults, *cantucci* can be served with black coffee for a mid-morning break or as a dessert after lunch or dinner, dipped in dessert wine, either sitting at the table or in front of a fireplace in winter, and in the garden or out on the terrace in the summer. For the children, cantucci can be enjoyed at any time of the day, as they are or dunked in hot or cold milk.

Torta Aromatica

Aromatic Cake

The following recipe was inspired by a *Torta del pastore* (Shepherd's cake) recipe that also features liqueur sourced from the Tuscan-based distillery Borsi Liquori. I have used a bittersweet orange-flavoured liqueur called Amarancia, and added some vanilla essence to enrich the *torta*'s aroma, while the original Shepherd's cake uses Liquore del Pastore (Shepherd's Liqueur), a lemon and vanilla preparation.

As both liqueurs have a relatively low alcohol content and as the baking stage cooks out most if not all of the alcohol, while retaining the citrus fragrance and flavour, this cake is suitable for both adults and children to enjoy.

In my opinion, the best orange or lemon liqueur to use for this cake is one from the award-winning Borsi distillery, which you can buy from the adjoining store in Castagneto Carducci in Tuscany, should you happen to pass it, or via the Internet, if you are not so lucky... Alternatively, you could use orange blossom essence – but, if I were you, I would go to Tuscany!

Suitable for children and adults
Preparation time: 20 minutes (plus overnight flavouring)
Cooking time: 35–40 minutes
Serves 8–10 people

What you need

400 g / 14 oz ricotta cheese
2 tbsp Amarancia orange liqueur or orange
    blossom essence
300 g / 10½ oz / 1½ US cups white caster / superfine sugar
30 ml / 1 fl oz / 2 tbsp extra-virgin olive oil
300 g / 10½ oz / 2⅔ US cups white plain / all-purpose flour
16 g / ½ oz / 4½ US tsp baking powder
1 tbsp vanilla essence

How you make it

In a large mixing bowl, blend the cheese and the orange blossom essence (or liqueur). Cover with cling film / plastic wrap and leave it to flavour in the fridge overnight.

On the following day, take the ricotta out of the fridge and bring it back to room temperature.

Pre-heat the oven to 180°C / 350°F / Gas Mark 4.

Add the sugar to the ricotta and mix well. Pour the extra-virgin olive oil and mix well. Sift the flour into the mixture and mix well. Add the baking powder and mix well.

Butter and sprinkle with flour a spring / spring form cake tin (24 cm / 9½ in diameter).

Gently pour the mixture into the cake tin.

Bake for 35 to 40 minutes until the top is golden.

6

Le feste

Special occasions

This chapter is dedicated to the many events and festivities that see Italians gather around large tables with family and friends to celebrate together. *Le feste* (special occasions) are a wonderful 'excuse' to rejoice with plenty of delicious food, fine wine and delightful company.

It wouldn't have felt right to work on this chapter of celebrations on my own, so... I asked chef Attilio (Tito) Bergamaschi to help with the presentation of some of the recipes I have been both enjoying and cooking since I was a child. I also tested the Easter lamb recipe in good company by serving it to the merry Pignano community, with the assistance of the kitchen team.

Each dish has been created using seasonal, fresh and simple ingredients, enhancing natural flavours without over complicating them. Special occasions should be enjoyable for the cook, too, and shouldn't be stressful or demanding; otherwise, what kind of party would *that* be?!

Menù della Festa della Mamma

Mother's Day Menu

Mother's Day is celebrated all over the world. In Italy, the second Sunday of May is devoted to this festivity, as it is for many European countries. Same applies to the USA, where, in 1870, the pacifist Julia Ward Howe wrote her *Mother's Day Proclamation* in response to the brutalities of the American Civil War and the Franco-Prussian War and in support of all mothers whose sons had died in battle.

In European countries, such as the UK, Mother's Day has become synonymous with the Christian festival Mothering Sunday, which falls on the fourth Sunday in Lent. In Italy, too, Mother's Day has developed from both religion and secular traditions. The Catholic Church's May devotions to the Blessed Virgin Mary originated in Italy, as did May crowning, in which a crown, often made of spring flowers, is used to adorn a likeness of Mary to honour her status as the Mother of Jesus Christ.

A mother bears a new life as spring brings to the world blossom and renewed existence. The link between motherhood and nature sees flowers as symbols of Mary's divine maternity, carnations have been associated with the US holiday since its inception and, more broadly, flowers are 'children' of Mother Earth and will make an exquisite bouquet for your own mother or mother figure.

The following menu has been planned using recipes that even younger children can cook as a treat for their mother. Three of this book's 'stars' helped to prepare the dishes: Sofia (age 7) made the starter, Tania (12) made the main course and Nicoletta (9) made the dessert! This is a sophisticated menu that will surprise and delight mother and be enjoyed by the whole family.

Menu

Antipasto (starter)

Insalata di Valeriana, Riccia, Germogli di Piselli, Piselli Freschi e Mozzarella di Bufala

Lamb's Lettuce, Curly Endive, Pea Shoots, Garden Peas and Buffalo Mozzarella Salad

———

Secondo (main course)

Linguine al Pesce Mediterraneo

Linguine With Mediterranean Fish

———

Dolce (dessert)

Pera allo Sciroppo Aromatico con Mascarpone e Pistacchi

Pear in Aromatic Syrup with Mascarpone and Pistachio Nuts

Insalata di Valeriana, Riccia, Germogli di Piselli, Piselli Freschi e Mozzarella di Bufala

Lamb's Lettuce, Curly Endive, Pea Shoots, Garden Peas and Buffalo Mozzarella Salad

Suitable for adults and children
Preparation time: 15 minutes
Serves 4–6 people

What you need
100 g / 3½ oz lamb's lettuce / corn salad / valerian
    (*valeriana*, *songino*)
100 g / 3½ oz curly endive / frisée
100 g / 3½ oz pea shoots / pea tendrils / dau miu
100 g / 3½ oz fresh garden / green peas
400 g / 14 oz Buffalo mozzarella
a generous pinch of salt
75 ml / 2½ fl oz / 5 tbsp extra-virgin olive oil

Optional:
balsamic vinegar glaze (a very thick balsamic vinegar cream;
    my favourite is the fig version, for its sweetness)

How you make it
Wash and pat dry the salad leaves and the peas. Place them either into a large serving bowl or onto individual plates.

Tear the Buffalo mozzarella and lay on the salad.

Dress with salt, extra-virgin olive oil and cream of balsamic vinegar, if desired.

Linguine al Pesce Mediterraneo

Linguine with Mediterranean Fish

Suitable for adults and children
Preparation time: 15 minutes
Cooking time: 15 minutes
Serves 4–6 people

What you need

4 litres / 135 fl oz / 17 US cups water
1 large red onion, peeled and chopped
300 g / 10½ oz fresh tomatoes (choose from baby plum,
   Roma plum cherry, campari, etc.)
½ bunch fresh flat-leaf parsley
1 tbsp salted capers
2 whole cloves garlic, peeled
120 ml / 4 fl oz / 8 tbsp extra-virgin olive oil
3 medium cod fillets, skinned
5 g / 1 tsp (half a palmful) coarse sea salt
400 g / 14 oz dry linguine (or substitute with spaghetti)
5 tbsp taggiasche olives (or substitute with other black
   or green olive varieties)
salt
black pepper, freshly ground (if desired)

How you make it

Bring the water to boil in a large saucepan.

Chop the onion, the tomatoes and the parsley and set to one side in separate bowls.

Wash the capers in cold running water and set to one side.

Peel the garlic.

Pour 5 tablespoons of extra-virgin olive oil in a large saucepan. Add the onion and the garlic and gently fry for 3 minutes. Add the cod fillets and cook for 5 minutes. Add the tomatoes, the olives and the capers and cook for a further 5 minutes, stirring occasionally so that the fish starts breaking into small pieces.

Meanwhile, once the pasta water reaches boiling point, add the sea salt and then add the linguine. When the pasta is cooked al dente (follow the packet instructions), drain it.

Add the linguine to the fish sauce and mix for a couple of minutes.

Add the chopped parsley, the remaining olive oil and serve immediately.

Grind some black pepper over the top of the dish, if desired.

Pera allo Sciroppo Aromatico con Mascarpone e Pistacchi

Pear in Aromatic Syrup with Mascarpone and Pistachio Nuts

Suitable for adults and children
Preparation time: 10 minutes
Cooking time: 35–40 minutes
Serves 4–6 people

What you need

4–6 medium dessert pears
1 vanilla pod
700 ml / 23½ fl oz / 3 US cups water
50 g / 1¾ oz / ¼ US cup demerara / raw sugar
1 cinnamon stick
1 tbsp dry rose petals (available from a spice market or
    similar specialist outlets)
¼ lemon
4–6 tsp acacia honey
4–6 scoops mascarpone (or substitute with double (heavy)
    cream or crème fraîche)
4–6 tsp peeled pistachio nuts

How you make it

Wash the pears. Slit the vanilla pod. Place the pears in a medium-sized saucepan (with a lid, used later) and add all the ingredients except the honey, the mascarpone and the pistachio nuts.

Bring to the boil on a medium heat (approximately 10 minutes). When the syrup boils, lower the heat to the minimum, cover with a lid and simmer for a further 20 to 25 minutes, until the pears are soft. Make sure that, every so often, you spoon some of the syrup onto the pears to flavour them.

Serve each pear in a single bowl. Pour some of the (strained) syrup over each pear. Add one tablespoonful of mascarpone and a teaspoonful of crushed pistachio nuts to each. Drizzle with a teaspoon of honey.

Serve immediately.

Menù del Compleanno

Birthday Menu

Perhaps as far back as 3,000 or even 4,000 years ago, an ancient Egyptian Pharaoh is thought to have enjoyed a birthday 'festival', including a sumptuous meal, although it may in fact have been a celebration of his coronation and so his 'birth' as a king. In ancient Rome, the birthdays of family members and friends were honoured with banquets and gift giving – as were the birthdays of past and present emperors, temples, towns... in fact, any excuse for a party, it would seem!

The origin of the birthday cake – specifically, one decorated with candles – may be traced back to the ancient Greeks who honoured Artemis, goddess of the moon, through the offering of a round, moon-shaped honey cake that featured candles, perhaps to represent the glowing moon or to send prayers and good wishes up through the wisps of smoke.

Travelling in time through to medieval customs, another theory is that the tradition of the birthday cake started in Germany with a sweet bread shaped as a swaddled baby Jesus Christ to celebrate his birth. This cake, with a single candle placed in the middle to signify the 'light of life', would come to be used to mark all children's birthdays.

However the celebrations or the customary foods associated with them came about, I hope that you and your family and friends will enjoy your birthday with this menu. *Buon compleanno*, as we say in Italy!

Menu

Antipasti (starters)

Croquettes di Patate della Nonna

Granny's Best Potato Croquettes

**Frittelle di Prosciutto e Fontina
(o di Scamorza e Speck)**

Ham & Cheese (or Scamorza & Speck)
Pastry Parcels

Secondo (main course)

Polpettone con Porri Saltati

Polpettone with Sautéed Leeks

Dolce (dessert)

Budino Freddo al Cioccolato

Cold Chocolate Pudding

Croquettes di Patate della Nonna

Granny's Best Potato Croquettes

This *antipasto – Secchielli di croquettes e frittelle* (Crispy croquettes and tasty pastry parcels) – combines two delicious dishes that can be served as finger-food with a celebratory aperitif or sitting around the table as *antipasto* and served with some tomatoes, crudités and olives. They work well together as party food for a buffet as well.

The *frittelle*, detailed in the next recipe, are perfect party-sized pastry parcels filled with tantalizing Italian cheeses and cured meats, while the recipe below is one born of the unconditional love that comes from grandmothers… If they are fortunate enough to live healthily and happily until a very old age, Italian grandmothers still do everything for their grandchildren, who, by this time, will have reached the age of 20 or even 30 years old, because these grandmothers are still doing everything for their own children, who are now in their 40s or 50s!

The *frittelle*, detailed in the next recipe, are perfect party-sized pastry parcels filled with tantalizing Italian cheeses and cured meats, while the recipe below is one born of the unconditional love that comes from grandmothers… If they are fortunate enough to live healthily and happily until a very old age, Italian grandmothers still do everything for their grandchildren, who, by this time, will have reached the age of 20 or even 30 years old, because these grandmothers are still doing everything for their own children, who are now in their 40s or 50s!

I have alluded, in this book's Introduction, to my *nonna*'s Wednesday banquets; practically the entire family was invited to enjoy not only her food but also her great company. We would listen to old stories and to *nonna* reciting librettos of operas – and sometimes singing and humming them. She was not the greatest vocalist, but had been going to the theatre regularly with her father since she was 11, when her mother died, passing on to her the honour and 'responsibility' of accompanying him to the opera.

These *Croquettes di Patate della Nonna* always remind me of those wonderful Wednesdays.

Suitable for adults and children
Preparation time: 50 minutes
Cooking time: 10 minutes
Serves 8 people

What you need
8 large potatoes
1 bunch fresh flat-leaf parsley, finely chopped
2 eggs
250 g / 8¾ oz / 2½ US cups parmesan, grated
salt
100 g / 3½ oz / ⅘ US cup white plain / all-purpose flour
abundant sunflower oil, to fry

How you make it
In a large saucepan, boil the potatoes (whole, with the skin on) for 35 to 40 minutes, depending on size, until soft.

In the meantime, chop the parsley finely.

Peel the potatoes and, using a potato ricer, create a mound in a large bowl. If you do not have a ricer, use a masher. With the ricer, though, the potato mix becomes fluffier.

Add the eggs, cheese, parsley and salt. Mix together.

Using your hands, form medium-sized cylinders shapes, approximately 4 to 5 cm (1½ to 2 in) each.

Roll the cylinders in flour until fully coated.

Heat the oil in a large frying pan. Fry the croquettes until golden brown. Place on a kitchen paper / paper towel to drain. Serve hot.

Versatility
While frying the croquettes, in order to keep hot those that had already been fried, good old granny use to store them between two plates on the kitchen radiator. If you have an AGA or a similar stored-heat stove and cooker, even better!

Frittelle di Prosciutto e Fontina (o di Scamorza e Speck)

Ham & Cheese (or Scamorza & Speck) Pastry Parcels

Suitable for adults and children
Preparation time: 50 minutes
Cooking time: 10 minutes
Serves 8–10 people

What you need
For the pastry:
1 kg / 2.2 lb / 10 US cups white plain / all-purpose flour,
    plus extra for dusting
300 ml / 10 fl oz / 1¼ US cups extra-virgin olive oil
4 eggs, beaten
a pinch of salt
30 ml / 1 fl oz / ⅛ US cup warm water
abundant sunflower oil, to fry

For the filling (see Versatility, below):
6 egg yolks
250 g / 8¾ oz ricotta cheese
250 g / 8¾ oz / 2½ US cups Fontina and / or scamorza
    cheese / *scamorza affumicata* (smoked scamorza), grated
200 g / 7 oz *prosciutto cotto* (Italian cooked ham) and / or
    speck (smoked cured ham), finely sliced
salt
pepper

How you make it
For the pastry:
Sieve the flour into a large bowl. Make a hole. Add the olive oil, the eggs, which have been beaten, a pinch of salt and the warm water.

Work the mixture with your hands until it forms a smooth dough. Leave it to rest for 30 minutes wrapped in a tea towel.

For the filling(s):
Mix the egg yolks with the ricotta. Grate the scamorza / Fontina cheese and add to the mixture. Slice finely the speck/ *prosciutto cotto* and add to the mixture. Add salt and pepper.

For the pastry parcels:
Roll out the dough and cut out circles and squares of 8 to 10 cm (3 to 4 in) each. Fill each circle/square with the filling fold over and seal. To make a perfect seal put some drops of water on the edge of the pastry.

In a large frying pan (use a deep fat / deep fryer if you have one), heat the sunflower oil. When hot, fry the *frittelle* on both sides until golden. Drain on kitchen paper / paper towels and serve hot.

Versatility
If you choose the *scamorza affumicata* and speck combination, the flavour will be smoky and intense. For a tasty but not quite so concentrated flavour, use Fontina and prosciutto… or, as I do all the time, make the *frittelle* with both flavour groupings, which should please everybody!

Polpettone con Porri Saltati

Polpettone with Sautéed Leeks

Polpettone is a classic recipe from the Padan Plain (*Pianura Padana*) in Lombardy, the regional capital of which is my hometown, Milan. I chose to include this recipe in the Special Occasions chapter because it is one of those dishes that my mother used to make either on Sundays or for a special occasion, as it is quite laborious.

Nevertheless, the time spent in the kitchen is well worth it, not only because *polpettone* (which is a little bit like a meatloaf) is absolutely delicious, but also because it lasts in the fridge for a few days and can be eaten hot or cold, used for filling panini or prepared in advance for buffets or parties. Freshly made tomato sauce poured over slices of leftover *polpettone* gives a totally different flavour to the dish, for example.

Suitable for adults and children
Preparation time: 60 minutes
Cooking time: depends on the thickness of your *polpettone*
    (never less than 30 minutes, maximum 50–60 minutes)
Serves 8 people

What you need

3 shallots, finely sliced
½ bunch fresh flat-leaf parsley, finely sliced
1 clove garlic, peeled and chopped
1 white bread roll, soft part scooped out
125 ml / 4 fl oz / ½ US cup milk
450 g / 1 lb extra-lean minced / ground pork
450 g / 1 lb minced / ground veal (or substitute with extra-
    lean minced / ground beef)
170 g / 6 slices *prosciutto cotto*
    (or substitute with cooked ham)
200 g / 7 oz / 2 US cups parmesan cheese, grated
a pinch of nutmeg
a pinch of salt
a pinch of ground black pepper
3 eggs
45 g / 1½ oz / scant ½ US cup breadcrumbs, dry
90 ml / 3 fl oz / 6 tbsp extra-virgin olive oil
750 g / 26½ oz spinach
4 medium carrots
30 g / 1 oz / ¼ stick butter
100 g / 3½ oz Fontina (or substitute with fontal cheese
    or Gruyère), sliced
1 bunch fresh rosemary, chopped
1 bunch fresh sage, chopped
1 tbsp water
250 ml / 8½ fl oz / 1 US cup hot vegetable stock
    (*see* page 218)
aluminium / kitchen foil

How you make it

For the meat mixture:

Finely slice the shallots and parsley and chop the garlic. Set to one side, each in separate small bowls.

Take the soft part of the bread out of the roll and soak it in the ½ cup of milk for 5 minutes.

Into a large mixing bowl, put the minced meat, 3 slices of *prosciutto cotto* (finely chopped), the finely chopped parsley, grated parmesan (leaving a handful to one side), nutmeg, salt, pepper and 1 egg and mix well with your hands.

Squeeze out the milk from the soaked bread, ensuring that no liquid remains or the *polpettone* will break during cooking. Add to the mixture and mix well.

Add 2 to 3 tablespoons of breadcrumbs and mix well. If you see that the mixture is too soft, add a little more of the breadcrumbs, but don't over do it, as too much breadcrumb mix will dry the meat mixture. Should you see that the meat mixture has dried because of excess breadcrumbs, add 1 egg.

Leave the meat mixture to rest.

For the filling:

Into a large frying pan, pour 2 tablespoons of extra-virgin olive oil and put on a low heat. When the oil is hot, place the spinach in the pan and wilt the leaves for a few minutes, adding salt and pepper. When the spinach is cooked, press with some kitchen paper / paper towels to make sure any liquid left is squeezed out. Set to one side.

Boil the carrots (whole) until *al dente*. They still have to be very firm. When they are cooked, pat dry to absorb any liquid and then slice them. Set to one side.

Optional:

Make an omelette and add it to the filling. Simply beat the remaining 2 eggs. Add salt, pepper, and a handful of grated parmesan cheese and mix well. In a frying pan, melt the butter and pour the egg mixture in. Cook until mixture becomes an omelette.

For the polpettone:

Cut enough aluminium / kitchen foil to wrap the *polpettone*.

Lay the meat mixture flat on the foil. Across it, layer the spinach, carrots, slices of ham and the sliced cheese (plus the omelette, if you have made one).

Carefully roll up, forming a cylinder of about approximately 10 cm (4 in).

Once you have firmly shaped your *polpettone*, take another sheet of foil and sprinkle some breadcrumbs over it. Transfer and then wrap the *polpettone* as a parcel and finish shaping it as a cylinder. Leave it to rest for 30 minutes.

Pre-heat the oven (electric or gas – do not use the fan function) at 200°C / 400°F / Gas Mark 6.

Into an oval-shaped casserole, put 4 tablespoons of extra-virgin olive oil, the rosemary, sage, sliced shallots, chopped garlic, a generous pinch of salt, ground black pepper and 1 tablespoon of water and gently fry until the shallots are soft.

Carefully open the parcel and remove the *polpettone*. Place it in the casserole and cook for 5 minutes until it colours, turning it so that it cooks evenly.

In a deep oven dish (approximately 10 × 25 cm (4 × 10 in); make sure the oven dish is much bigger than the *polpettone* as the *polpettone* should not touch its sides), lay some greaseproof / wax baking paper. Place the *polpettone* in the oven dish and pour the cooking juice over the top.

Place in the oven for 50–60 minutes. Every 10 to 15 minutes, pour a couple of spoonfuls of the hot vegetable stock onto the top side of the *polpettone*. While it is cooking in the oven, do not turn the *polpettone* as it will break.

Once the *polpettone* is cooked, let it cool down for 20 minutes before laying it on a serving plate. Slice the *polpettone* (if the *polpettone* is sliced when still hot it will crumble). Filter the cooking juice, heat it and pour it over the top of the sliced *polpettone* before serving.

Versatility

Polpettone is one of those dishes, like lasagne, for instance, that is actually even more delicious the day after it has been cooked, so you could make it the day before the special occasion. Simply slice it cold and then re-heat on the day you are serving it.

I suggested serving *polpettone* with sautéed leeks (see recipe, opposite), but other side dishes that complement this dish well are roast potatoes and a mixed leaf salad.

Porri Saltati
Sautéed Leeks

To accompany the *polpettone*, or to enjoy on their own!

Suitable for adults and children
Preparation time: 10 minutes
Cooking time: 10 minutes
Serves 8 people

What you need
8 medium leeks, trimmed
45 ml / 1½ fl oz / 3 tbsp extra-virgin olive oil
3–4 tbsp balsamic vinegar, to taste
coarse sea salt

How you make it
Trim and wash the leeks. Slice them in half. Pour the oil into a grill pan or a frying pan. Heat it at a low heat. When the oil is hot, turn up the heat to medium and add the leeks.

Using tongs, keep turning the leeks until they start to colour. Add some coarse sea salt and cook until tender.

Before serving, dress with balsamic vinegar and some freshly ground black pepper, to taste.

Budino Freddo al Cioccolato

Cold Chocolate Pudding

Budino is one of Italy's favourite puddings for children. Here, Tito and I have created a slightly sophisticated version of this old-fashioned dessert, which has been given the seal of approval by our 'chocolate expert', Ben. The other children who tasted it agree and even some adults have been seen secretly scraping the bowl!

Suitable for adults and children
Preparation time: 40 minutes (plus 1½ hours, minimum, of chilling time in the freezer)
Serves 8–10 people

What you need
For the budino:
400 g / 14 oz organic dark / bittersweet chocolate (70% cocoa solids), broken up
70 g / 2½ oz organic dark / bittersweet chocolate (85% cocoa solids), broken up
170 g / 6 oz / 1½ sticks unsalted butter, cut into small pieces
7 medium eggs
50 g / 1¾ oz / ¼ US cup golden caster / superfine sugar
100 g / 3½ oz organic white chocolate, half cut into small pieces and half grated (to decorate)

For the fruit compote:
600 g / 21 oz berries of your choice (e.g. strawberries, blueberries, blackberries, etc. – or a mixture), washed
150 g / 5½ oz / ¾ US cup demerara / turbinado / raw sugar
200 ml / 6¾ fl oz / ¾ US cup water

How you make it

For the budino:

Break the dark chocolate, cut the butter into small pieces and place both in a bowl.

Melt the chocolate and the butter by placing the bowl on top of a saucepan filled with water (a *bagno maria* / bain-marie). Boil the water on a medium to low heat for 10 minutes.

Using two more bowls, separate the yolks from the egg whites.

Mix half of the sugar with the egg yolks. Beat the mixture with a hand-held electric whisk until it turns a pale yellow.

Mix the other half of the sugar with the egg whites until it thickens, forming soft peaks. Try to turn the spoon upside-down; if the mixture does not fall, it is ready.

Check on the melting chocolate and butter mixture. If it has melted, remove from the heat, gently stir and leave it in the bowl to cool down until at room temperature.

In a large mixing bowl, gently stir the chocolate and butter mixture in with the beaten yolks.

Gently fold in a spoonful at a time of the egg whites. Tito suggests a chef's trick of stirring anticlockwise with one hand and turning the bowl clockwise with the other hand until the mixture reaches a smooth and light consistency. Make sure there are no lumps in the mixture.

Cut half of the white chocolate into small pieces and stir it in.

Line a mould with cling film / plastic wrap. Pour the mixture in the mould. Cover the mould with cling film / plastic wrap. Place in the freezer for 1½ hours.

Grate the remaining white chocolate, which you'll put on top of the *budino* to decorate at the moment of serving.

For the fruit compote:

Into a medium-sized saucepan, put the berries, sugar and water and let the mixture cook for 10 minutes, until the liquid thickens and the berries are soft.

Cool the compote down to room temperature before serving with the *budino*.

Serve the *budino* cold with grated white chocolate sprinkled over the top and the fruit compote at the side.

Versatility

If you are making the *budino* on the same day that you are going to eat it, take it out of the freezer 10 minutes before serving. If you make the *budino* the day before, take it out of the freezer half an hour before serving it.

L'estate di San Martino

Indian Summer

As noted in Chapter 4, 11 November is the feast day of Saint Martin (*La festa di San Martino*), and, at around the same time, when warmer weather follows the season's first freeze, *L'estate di San Martino* (the summer of Saint Martin, known more generally as an 'Indian summer') is observed. According to legend, Saint Martin gave his coat to a beggar who was suffering from the cold weather, hence his association with bringing warmth.

La festa di San Martino traditionally marked an important time for rural communities, when farming families would feast on the fruits of their autumn harvests, ahead of the leaner winter period. Chestnuts and wine remain, to this day, culinary indulgences associated with this ancient festival.

Our very close family friend Cristoforo used to make *Monte Bianco*, a sublime chestnut-based dessert, and I have had the great pleasure of making it with him thereby learning one of the 'secret' recipes of a family whose father we all remember being very partial to desserts. His wife Rosita and I were put in charge of peeling a mountain of chestnuts that Cristoforo then transformed into a confectionery work of art that, because of its shape and the copious amount of whipped cream used, recalls the Alpine mountain Mont Blanc. I am sharing this recipe with all the chestnut lovers.

Monte Bianco

Mont Blanc

Suitable for adults and children
Preparation time: 45 minutes
Cooking time: 40 minutes
Serves 4–6 people

What you need

1½ kg / 2¼ lb chestnuts, peeled
1½ litres / 51 fl oz / 6⅓ US cups whole (full-cream) milk
1–2 tbsp white sugar, according to taste
½ tsp salt
1 vanilla pod
150 g / 5¼ oz Amaretti (almond-flavoured) biscuits
250 g / 8½ fl oz / 1 US cup whipping cream / double (heavy) cream
1 heaped tbsp cocoa powder

How you make it

Peel the chestnuts. To make it easier taking the inner skin off, warm the chestnuts in the oven first, but at a low temperature to avoid roasting them.

Pour the milk into a large saucepan and add the peeled chestnuts. Add the sugar (1 or 2 tablespoons, depending on the sweetness of your tooth), the salt and the vanilla pod. Cook on a low heat for 30 to 40 minutes until the chestnuts are soft. Skim the milk while cooking.

Meanwhile, crumble the Amaretti biscuits and set to one side. To crumble the biscuits, I wrap them in a kitchen towel, folded in two, then crush them by rolling an empty glass bottle over the towel, so that the crumbs are not too fine and it stays uniform. If you don't want to follow this old-fashioned method and have a food processor, whizz the Amaretti in it for a few seconds.

Once the milk mixture has cooked, try it and adjust with sugar to taste. Allow the mixture to cool down. Strain the chestnuts, keeping some of the cooking milk to one side.

Using a food / vegetable mill, set on the middle size holes, purée the chestnuts together in a large bowl. The mixture should be smooth and soft. If it is not soft enough, add a little milk to it.

Using a potato ricer, purée the mixture once more, but this time directly onto the serving plate and shaping it into a mountain. Every time you purée one amount of chestnut mixture, sprinkle with some Amaretti crumbs.

Once the 'mountain' is made, whip the cream by using an electric hand-held whisk and a mixing bowl that has been kept in the fridge for 10 minutes beforehand. The colder the cream and the temperature of the mixing bowl, the better the cream will fluff up.

Spread the whipped cream on the 'mountain' from the bottom to the top. Decorate the top with either the rest of the Amaretti or cocoa powder.

Keep cool and serve within half an hour.

Il Pranzo di Natale

Christmas Lunch

In Italy, Christmas is commemorated in as many different ways as there are regions forming the country. In the north, it is celebrated on the morning of 25 December. Presents are opened, Mass is attended and lunch is served. Lunch runs into dinner, becoming one big banquet. In Milan, some churchgoers attend Midnight Mass on 24 December, after which the congregation will serve and together enjoy a customary hot chocolate. In southern Italy, Christmas dinner is served on Christmas Eve, with families and friends gathering around lavish tables until the small hours. After the midnight feast, which is usually a fish-based menu, presents are exchanged.

The Italian Christmas menu, too, varies from region to region, with many different culinary customs observed. Catholics from both northern and southern Italy, however, generally refrain from eating meat on Christmas Eve. Our menu, below, starts with an ambrosial aperitif that will please both adults and children with its heavenly combination of sweet, dry and sharp flavours all bubbling together. Fish and game is on the table to offer variety to the palate, along with seasonal, refined yet very easy to make side dishes. Dessert is a traditional panettone enriched with a luxurious cream. Alternatively, pandoro – a light, buttery cake generously dusted with icing / confectioner's sugar – may be enjoyed for its refined simplicity of taste. Fresh and dried fruit, roasted chestnuts, nougat, chocolates, fruit gelatins and sweets are also on offer, should anybody feel like indulging just a little more!

Another ritual observed on Christmas Eve, particularly during the times of Galeazzo Sforza up until the end of 1700, and, since then,

Menu

Aperitif

Aperitivo al Melograno

Pomegranate Aperitif

———

Antipasto (starter)

Tre Assaggi di Natale

Three-Fish Festive Tasters

———

Primo (soup, rice or pasta dish)

Quadrati di Natale

Christmas Squares

———

Secondo (main course)

**Faraona con Purè di Sedano Rapa
e Radicchio Grigliato all'Aceto Balsamico**

Guinea Fowl with Celeriac Mash and Grilled
Radicchio with Aged Balsamic Vinegar

———

Dolce (dessert)

Panettone con Crema al Mascarpone

Panettone with Mascarpone Cream Drizzle

sporadically practiced through the remaining centuries up to our times, sees the family gathered around the fireplace to burn a large log of wood with dry leaves and apples, throwing wine and juniper berries over the fire three times as an invitation for good fortune during the merry celebratory season.[1] The evocative and enveloping aroma of this roaring fire can still be replicated in modern-day family rituals when chestnuts are roasted and nibbled during the luxuriantly lazy and contented period that follows a sumptuous Christmas meal. In 1996, when my husband and I were newly wed, we spent Christmas by Lake Como with my extended family, who hosted a bounteous banquet comprising seafood and fish starters, homemade tortellini in capon broth, risotto, pheasant in a peaches and cream sauce, guinea fowl accompanied by various seasonal vegetables, clementine sorbet and, to finish, a panettone filled with vanilla and chocolate gelato... it was a very 'satisfactory' meal! A few hours after its conclusion, we all gathered around the fireplace, comfortably ensconced in armchairs and sofas as we watched my uncle make a fire and perform the old ritual. Chestnuts were roasted and, in spite of the protests, excuses and refusals, the big pile of chestnuts 'vanished' as if into the darkness of the past centuries!

1   Verri, P. (1783) *Storia di Milano*. Available at Milan Digital Library, www.digitami.it; accessed November 2011. Milan: Stamperia di Guiseppe Marelli.

Aperitivo al Melograno

Pomegranate Aperitif

The pomegranate is a motif often found in religious decoration and its ruby-red juice is a wonderfully refreshing way to begin Christmas celebrations. Adults and children alike can enjoy this luscious aperitif as it can be made with sparkling water or with sparkling wine. *Buon Natale*!

Suitable for adults and children
Preparation time: 15 minutes
Serves 16 (8 with alcohol, 8 without)

What you need
50 g / 1¾ oz / ¼ US cup granulated / white sugar
500 ml / 17 fl oz / 2 US cups water
3 medium pomegranates, juice of
1 bottle Prosecco wine, chilled
1 bottle sparkling / soda water, chilled

How you make it
Mix the sugar with the water to make a syrup. The quantities can be changed according to the sharpness of the pomegranate and to your taste. The important thing to remember is to use equal measures of water and sugar to make the syrup.

Spoon out the juicy red seeds / grains of the pomegranates. Whizz them in a food processor for a few minutes. Pour through a sieve to obtain the juice. Add the syrup to sweeten the taste if needed.

Pour the pomegranate juice (mixed with the syrup) at the bottom of each glass.

Carefully pour the Prosecco, for the adults, and the sparkling / soda water, for the children, into each glass.

Gently stir and serve immediately.

Tre Assaggi di Natale

Three-Fish Festive Tasters

This starter can be served either with the aperitif, if you want to start your celebration in a more informal way, or at the table when the party is seated.

Suitable for adults and children
Preparation time: 30 minutes
Makes 18 'tasters'

What you need

For the salmon tasters:
3 slices sourdough / naturally leavened bread,
    halved and toasted
butter, for the toast
½ small bunch fresh dill, finely chopped
250 g / 8 oz smoked salmon
1 scoop double (heavy) cream
½ lemon, juice of
2 pink pepper peppercorns, whole

For the cod tasters:
3 slices sourdough / naturally leavened bread,
    halved and toasted
2 cloves garlic, peeled
75 ml / 2½ fl oz / 5 tbsp extra-virgin olive oil
250 g / 8 oz cod fillet (sustainably sourced), skinned
a pinch of salt
1 scoop double (heavy) cream
½ lemon, juice of
black pepper, freshly ground
½ small bunch fresh flat-leaf parsley, finely chopped
100 g / 3½ oz pitted Niçoise or taggiasche olives
    (or substitute with oven-cooked black olives)

For the tuna tasters:
3 slices sourdough / naturally leavened bread,
    halved and toasted
75 ml / 2½ fl oz / 5 tbsp extra-virgin olive oil
250 g / 8 oz white tuna (sustainably sourced), glass jar of
1 tbsp double (heavy) cream
½ lemon, juice of
1 tbsp chopped fresh flat leaf parsley
black pepper, freshly ground
20–30 salted capers, rinsed thoroughly in
    cold running water

How you make it

For the salmon tasters:
Halve the slices of bread. Toast and butter them. Chop the dill and set to one side.

Put the smoked salmon, the double (heavy) cream, the lemon juice and the peppercorns in a food processor and whizz to obtain a smooth paste.

Spread the paste over the bread, sprinkle with the chopped dill and serve.

For the cod tasters:
Halve the slices of bread and toast them. Rub the bread with 1 peeled clove of garlic. Drizzle with 2 tablespoons of extra-virgin olive oil.

Into a frying pan, put a spoonful of extra-virgin olive oil, the other clove of garlic, finely chopped, and the cod fillet on a medium heat, turning frequently until the cod is cooked. Add a pinch of salt.

In a food processor, using the 'pulse' mode, blend the cod, the cream, the lemon juice, salt, pepper, the parsley and 2 tablespoons extra-virgin olive oil. You want to retain a bit of texture in the paste. If the paste is too thick, add an additional drizzle of olive oil and mix.

Spread the paste over the bread and decorate each piece with an olive.

For the tuna tasters:
Halve the slices of bread and toast them. Drizzle some extra-virgin olive oil. Drain the oil from the tuna in the jar.

Put all the ingredients in a food processor and blend into a paste choosing your preferred texture.

Spread the paste and decorate with a couple of capers.

Quadrati di Natale

Christmas Squares

This is a rich *primo* but with a delicate flavour. Add or omit the salmon roe according to preference.

If you wish to make your own pasta, simply follow the recipe below; otherwise, buy 600 g / 1 lb 5 oz of fresh lasagna sheets from an Italian deli or good quality supermarket. In either case, you will need to cut the sheets of pasta into squares that fit your pasta bowl size.

Suitable for adults and children
Preparation time: varies (for fresh pasta, 75 minutes; if you are using fresh sheets of lasagne, 20 minutes)
Cooking time: 10 minutes
Serves 8 people

What you need
4 litres / 135 fl oz / 17 US cups water
5 g / 1 tsp (half a palmful) coarse sea salt

For fresh pasta:
500 g / 17½ oz / 4 US cups flour for making pasta (type 00, *dopio zero*) (or substitute with plain white flour)
1 whole egg
10 egg yolks

For the sauce:
1 tbsp fresh flat-leaf parsley, chopped
3 tbsp fresh chives, chopped
100 g / 3½ oz / 1 stick unsalted butter
300 ml / 10 fl oz / 1¼ US cups double (heavy) cream
700 g / 1½ lb fresh wild salmon fillets
salt
4 pink peppercorns, crushed (use more if you like your food peppery)
extra-virgin olive oil, to dress

Optional:
150 g / 5½ oz salmon roe

How you make it
For the fresh pasta:
Sieve the flour onto a cold surface (metal or marble works best). Make a well in the centre, add the egg and the egg yolks. Knead the dough with your hands until it becomes firm and doesn't stick to your fingers anymore.

Wrap it in cling film / plastic wrap and put it in the fridge for 30–40 minutes to rest.

With the aid of a pasta machine, start working the rested pasta dough, gradually going down to the lowest degree of thickness. Fold the stretched dough the same width of your pasta machine, turn it 90 degrees and repeat the procedure until the pasta dough feels smooth.

Cut the dough into squares that fit your pasta bowl size.

For the sauce:
Chop the parsley and the chives and keep to one side in separate bowls.

In a large non-stick frying pan, melt the butter on a low heat and add the double (heavy) cream. Add the salmon, a pinch of salt, the crushed pink peppercorns, the parsley and cook for 5 minutes. Keep warm.

For the Christmas squares:
Bring a large saucepan filled with water to the boil.

Warm the pasta bowls in the oven so that when you serve the food it stays hot for longer.

When the water reaches boiling point, add the sea salt and then add the pre-cut pasta squares and cook for 3 to 4 minutes. Gently drain the pasta, making sure not to break the squares.

In each pasta bowl, lay a square of pasta, then add a spoonful of sauce. Alternate between the pasta and the sauce layers, finishing with the sauce on top. Drizzle a little bit of olive oil over each, and sprinkle with chives and the salmon roe, to taste.

Faraona con Purè di Sedano Rapa e Radicchio Grigliato all'Aceto Balsamico

Guinea Fowl with Celeriac Mash and Grilled Radicchio with Aged Balsamic Vinegar

Suitable for adults and children
Preparation time: 30 minutes
Cooking time: 70 minutes
Serves 6–8 people

What you need
For the guinea fowl:
1 free-range guinea fowl, whole
50 g / 1¾ oz / ½ stick butter
1 bulb garlic, crushed
25 cl (250 ml) / 8½ fl oz dry white wine
1 bunch fresh sage
30 ml / 1 fl oz / 2 tbsp extra-virgin olive oil
1 lemon, quartered
1 dried chilli

How you make it
For the guinea fowl:
Pre-heat the oven to 190°C / 375°F / Gas Mark 5.

Wash the guinea fowl. Make some little cuts in the skin. Put some butter between the skin and the flesh to add moisture and flavour once the fowl is cooked.

Put the guinea fowl breast side up in an oven tray. Add all the other ingredients. Cover the oven tray with aluminium / kitchen foil and put it in the oven for 30 minutes.

Take the guinea fowl out of the oven, turn it breast side down and put it back in the oven without the foil. Brush the guinea fowl with its own juice from time to time to make sure that the meat doesn't dry. Cook for another 15–20 minutes until it colours on this side.

Turn the guinea fowl breast side up again and cook for a further 15 minutes until the skin is crisp.

Purè di Sedano Rapa
Celeriac Mash

Radicchio Grigliato all'Aceto Balsamico
Grilled Radicchio with Aged Balsamic Vinegar

What you need
3 medium heads celeriac, peeled and diced
salt
pepper
30 ml / 1 fl oz / 2 tbsp extra-virgin olive oil

Optional:
2 tbsp fresh flat-leaf parsley (if desired), chopped

How you make it
Peel and dice the celeriac.

Bring a medium-sized saucepan of salted water to the boil. Add the celeriac and cook on a low heat until soft for about 15 to 20 minutes.

Once cooked, mash the celeriac using a potato masher or a rolling pin. Drizzle with extra-virgin olive oil, season with salt and pepper and mix well. Add parsley if desired.

What you need
2 medium heads of radicchio / red chicory
    (preferabley Trevisano or Chioggia varieties if available),
    cut into wedges
100 ml / 3⅓ fl oz / ½ US cup extra-virgin olive oil
salt
black pepper, freshly ground
aged balsamic vinegar (or substitute with balsamic vinegar
    glaze, which has a much thicker consistency)

How you make it
Wash the radicchio and cut into wedges.

Lay on a plate and dress with a generous drizzle of olive oil, salt and pepper.

Grill the radicchio using a grill-pan or lightly fry using a non-stick frying pan, depending on which you have available. Cook for approximately 10 minutes. Using tongs, constantly turn the radicchio until it browns. Add balsamic vinegar and let it evaporate for a few minutes.

Serve hot or at room temperature, as you prefer.

Versatility
To serve *Faraona con puré di sedano rapa e radicchio grigliato all'aceto balsamico*, simply lay the guinea fowl, the celeriac mash and the radicchio on a serving plate and drizzle with your best extra-virgin olive oil. Serve hot.

Panettone con Crema al Mascarpone

Panettone with Mascarpone Cream Drizzle

Panettone is a classic Milanese Christmas cake that has become the archetypal Italian Christmas cake all over the world. Nowadays hardly anybody makes it at home, but freshly made, artisan panettone is widely available in patisseries while commercially produced panettone can be quite good, too, provided you choose a high quality brand. The classic recipe features sultanas and orange peel, but you can also find versions without orange peel and a version that includes chocolate chips.

Pandoro is another very famous Italian Christmas cake, this one originating from Verona. It is a very light cake dusted with icing / confectioner's sugar. To make the most of the softness of this cake, keep it next to a source of heat before serving it. We used to put pandoro on a radiator for an hour prior to serving.

Panettone is served either on its own or with the delicious mascarpone cream presented below. In some patisseries in Milan and its surrounding province you can even find panettone filled with *gelato*!

Versatility
After panettone and/or pandoro are served, dry fruit, roasted chestnuts, fresh fruit, chocolate and sweets are offered

Suitable for adults and children
Preparation time: 10 minutes
Serves 6 people

What you need
500 g / 1 lb 1 oz mascarpone
3 eggs, yolks and whites separated
50 g / 4 tbsp / ½ oz granulated sugar

How you make it
Keep the ingredients cold until the moment of using them.

Separate the egg yolks and whites, making sure that no egg yolk accidentally falls into the egg whites. Should this happen, the egg whites will not become stiff.

Using a hand-held whisk, beat the yolks with the sugar until the mixture turns a pale yellow colour.

Wash and thoroughly dry the hand whisk, as any water left will prevent the egg whites from stiffing. Then, in a separate bowl, beat the egg whites. Whisk until they form soft peaks.

Using a spatula, gently fold in the mascarpone and stir with care. Be careful not to over-stir the mascarpone or it will turn into a butter.

Gently fold the egg whites in the yolk and mascarpone mix, stirring until you obtain a smooth cream.

Store the cream in the fridge until you are ready to serve it.

Versatility
As a variation for children, add 1 tablespoon of cocoa powder or 1 teaspoon of cinnamon. As an optional addition for adults, add 1 tablespoon of cognac / whisky or 1 teaspoon of finely ground coffee powder.

Carnevale

Carnival

Carnevale is synonymous with cakes and sweets and, in general, of 'being naughty'. The 'opulent' cakes eaten during the festival historically mark the period before the restraint of Lent, in preparation for Easter. During *carnevale*, indulgences such as rich fried cakes coated with sugar or honey are commonly enjoyed.

The festival may date as far back as 1094, and very likely to Roman times – after all, who better than the Romans to know how to indulge and enjoy themselves? It is also thought that, in order to keep the masses under control and gratified, street parties were permitted every now and again to appease any discontent. Dancing, singing and feasting were the main means of entertainment. From this idea, centuries later, came the *Carnevale di Venezia* (Carnival of Venice), in which, as well as street dancing and singing, masks became a central component. Wearing a mask helped everyone to disguise their identity, and, in this way, social differences were dispensed with and behaviours disinhibited.

Cakes and masks are still potent symbols of the Italian *carnevale*, which is celebrated between February and March, depending on when Easter Sunday falls in the yearly calendar. Different regions have various names and preparations for similar celebratory cakes. I have here chosen a fragrant, crumbly, biscuit-like cake that is made all over Italy but is known by a variety of names, depending on which region you find yourself celebrating *carnevale*. You will find *chiacchiere* in Milan, *cenci* in Florence and *frappe* in Rome.

Chiacchiere di Carnevale

Crispy Carnival Cakes

Each region has a different name for these sweet, light, golden-fried delicacies, from *chiacchiere* in Milan, to *cenci* in Tuscany and *frappe* in Rome.

Suitable for adults and children
Preparation time: 45 minutes
Cooking time: 10 minutes
Serves 8 people

What you need

500 g / 17½ oz / 4 US cups white plain / all-purpose flour
50 g / 1¾ oz / ½ stick butter, diced and softened
4 eggs
100 g / 3½ oz / ½ US cup granulated / white sugar
4 cl (40 ml) / 1½ fl oz dry white wine
1 lemon, grated zest of
a pinch of salt
abundant sunflower oil, to fry
icing / confectioner's sugar, to decorate

How you make it

On a clean surface, sift the flour and form a mound. Make a hole and put the softened and diced butter in the middle. Beat the eggs with the sugar and add to the mixture.

Start working the dough. Add the wine, gradually, to make the dough soft and smooth.

Add the grated lemon zest and a pinch of salt. Keep working the dough until smooth and elastic. Shape into a ball and wrap in cling film / plastic wrap. Leave to rest for 30 minutes.

With a rolling pin, roll out the dough on a floured surface, as thinly as you can. Cut the rolled out dough into strips 3 cm (1¼ in) wide. If you wish, pinch each strip in the middle to shape it as a bow tie. Fry in deep, hot oil until lightly golden, constantly turning the *chiacchiere* so that they do not burn. Lay on kitchen paper / paper towels to drain the oil.

When cooled, sprinkle each strip with abundant icing / confectioner's sugar and serve.

Versatility

Cenci and *frappe* are thicker than *chiacchiere*, so when you roll out the dough decide if you prefer a thin or thick biscuit-like consistency. In either case, they shouldn't be more than 10 mm / ⅓ in thick.

Menù di Pasqua

Easter Menu

The celebration of Easter coincides with the arrival of spring. Flowers and vegetables awake from the long winter in a joyful rebirth and it is a time of rebirth for nature as much as, for Christians, the rebirth of Jesus Christ. A strong spirituality allied to the observance of the Catholic faith is still felt in present-day Italy, as evidenced through *Via Crucis* (Stations of the Cross) on Good Friday, processions, Easter Sunday Mass announced by exultant bells and *Pasquetta* (Easter Monday) observances through the Easter holiday.

Lamb – religiously, the symbol of the body of Christ – is traditionally present on the Italian Easter table, although, in some regions, kid is served instead. Fresh lettuces and edible flowers adorn the main course. Eggs, embodying 'new life', are always a feature, having been boiled and their shell painted by children, or being made of chocolate or sugar. Eggs were forbidden during the strict observance of Lent in the past centuries, but have since been joyfully welcomed back as symbol of growing life at Easter. A *colomba* – a soft and light cake baked in the shape of a dove – is for Easter what the panettone is for Christmas. A *colomba* brings peace to the family, as the dove reflects the emblem of peace throughout the world.

In my Easter menu, however, I suggest a more regional dessert: *pastiera Napoletana* (Neapolitan Easter cake) is something for cake connoisseurs, and, as it is not commercially well known, it is a truly homemade cake. Every Neapolitan woman who can cook will claim to have the best, the original, the one and only recipe for *pastiera* as this cake dates back many centuries. It is steeped in legends harking back to pagan times after which it was adopted by the Catholic nuns of the convent of

Antipasto (starter)

Indivia a Sorpresa

Chicory Surprise

Secondo (main course)

Linguine al Pesce Mediterraneo

Linguine with Mediterranean Fish

Dolce (dessert)

Pastiera Napoletana

Neopolitan Easter Cake

San Gregorio Armeno, who used to make *pastiera* for the wealthy and powerful Neapolitan families at Easter time. The intense fragrance of this cake evokes the fresh scent of flowers blossoming at springtime, when life on Earth blooms.

Buona Pasqua, as we would say in Italy to wish you all Happy Easter!

Indivia a Sorpresa

Chicory Surprise

Suitable for adults and children
Preparation time: 15 minutes
Serves 6 people

What you need
5 eggs, hard-boiled and peeled
chicory / Belgian endive
250 g / 8¾ oz cream cheese
    (or substitute with quark cheese)
a pinch of salt
white pepper, freshly ground
1 bunch fresh chives, finely choppped

How you make it
Hard-boil the eggs. Peel them and leave them to cool.

Wash and pat dry the chicory / Belgian endive.

Using a fork, crumble the eggs and mix them with the cream
cheese. Add a pinch of salt and, if desired, the pepper. Mix
well until the mixture is creamy.

Fill each leaf of endive with one spoonful of the mixture.

Finely chop the chives and sprinkle over the top. Lay out on a
serving plate.

Agnello in Salsa Gialla con Patate Dorate e Songino

Lamb in Yellow Sauce with Golden Potatoes and Lambs Lettuce

For this recipe, you could substitute lamb with kid goat / cabrito. Kid is a bit leaner as a meat than lamb, but in terms of taste they are pretty similar. In Italy, it is a question of regional choice; for instance, in Sardinia, kid goat is very popular.

The *salsa gialla* (yellow sauce) is presented as two versions. One was inspired by a suggestion made by my daughters' godfathers Giorgio and Stephen – gourmands, or, as seen through a child's eye, 'gluttons', as this version is quite creamy! The other version has a stronger lemon flavour, which enhances very well the mild kid goat meat.

Suitable for adults and children
Preparation time: 45 minutes
Cooking time: 1 hour
Serves 6 people

What you need

For the stock:
1 small carrot, peeled and chopped
1 small celery stick, chopped
1 small onion, peeled and halved
30 ml / 1 fl oz / 2 tbsp extra-virgin olive oil
400 ml / 13½ fl oz / 1¾ US cups water
salt
4 peppercorns
200 ml / 6¾ fl oz / ¾ US cup milk

For the lamb:
1 kg / 2¼ lb lamb (or substitute with kid)
60 ml / 2 fl oz / 4 tbsp extra-virgin olive oil
1 bunch fresh rosemary
1 bunch fresh sage
10 juniper berries
2 cloves garlic, peeled and whole

For the sauce:
30 g / 1 oz / ¼ stick butter
30 g white plain / all-purpose flour
500 ml / 17 fl oz / 2 US cups milk
a pinch of salt
white pepper, ground
a pinch of nutmeg, freshly grated (to taste)
2 lemons, freshly squeezed juice of
2 eggs

To decorate:
1 bunch of fresh flat-leaf parsley, finely chopped
¼ lemon, grated zest of

How you make it

Pre-heat the oven to 180°C / 350°F / Gas Mark 4.

Peel and wash the vegetables. Halve the onion. Heat up a small non-stick frying pan and, when hot, place the halved onion flat side down to brown for two minutes.

Chop the rest of the vegetables and place them with the onion and two tablespoons of extra-virgin olive oil in a small saucepan. Cook on a medium heat for about two minutes, stirring constantly. Pour the water in and bring to the boil. When the stock reaches boiling point, lower the heat and simmer for 15 minutes. Then add a pinch of salt and the 4 peppercorns. Pour the milk in the stock, stir well and turn the heat off. Keep the stock warm covered with a lid.

Cut the lamb into pieces. In a large casserole, which can be transferred to the oven, pour 4 tablespoons of extra-virgin olive oil, place the rosemary, the sage, the juniper berries, the garlic and cook on a low heat for 2 minutes. Place the lamb in the casserole, turn the heat to medium and brown for about 3 minutes, constantly turning the pieces of lamb to reach an even colour. Add a ladle of the stock/milk mixture. Transfer to the oven.

Bake for 40 minutes.

Halfway the cooking time, turn the pieces of lamb so that they cook evenly. Check that the lamb does not dry and pour some of its own cooking juice onto the lamb. Add a little more stock/milk mixture, if necessary.

Make the béchamel / white sauce. In a small saucepan, melt the butter, then remove from heat and stir in the flour. Slowly add half the milk, stirring gently, then stir in the rest. Keep stirring on low heat until boiling. When it boils, gently cook for 1 to 2 minutes. Add salt, pepper and nutmeg to your taste. Remove the sauce from the heat leaving it in the saucepan.

Squeeze the lemons to obtain the juice. Beat the eggs and mix well with the lemon juice. Slowly pour the mixture into the white sauce, stirring constantly and quickly to avoid the egg clotting. When the ingredients are blended in, pour the yellow sauce onto the lamb.

Finely chop the parsley, grate a little lemon zest and sprinkle on the lamb to decorate. Serve hot.

Versatility

An alternative, more lemony and less creamy sauce can be prepared to accompany the lamb or kid meat as follows.

2 egg yolks
2 lemons, freshly squeezed juice of
a pinch of salt
white pepper, ground
a pinch of nutmeg, freshly grated
half a bunch flat-leaf parsley, finely chopped

Beat the egg yolks and leave to one side. Squeeze the juice of the two lemons and gently incorporate to the egg, a little at a time, stirring constantly. Add salt, pepper and nutmeg and mix together. Pour the mixture in a little saucepan and gently heat. Using a hand whisk, stir constantly and quickly to avoid the egg clotting. After 2 to 3 minutes, when the sauce thickens, turn the heat off. Either serve the sauce poured on the meat or to the side.

Patate Dorate
Golden Potatoes

What you need
120 ml / 4 fl oz / 8 tbsp extra-virgin olive oil
1 tbsp dried mixed herbs
1 bunch rosemary, shredded
6 garlic cloves, skin on, crushed
6 medium to large potatoes, unpeeled / skin still on
a pinch of salt
coarse sea salt

How you make it
Pre-heat the oven to 190°C / 375°F / Gas Mark 5.

Pour the olive oil on an oven tray, add the dry herbs and then shred the bunch of rosemary into the tray, pressing the leaves with a knife (to release their oils / flavour). Crush the garlic, leaving the skin on, and add to the oven tray. Put the tray in the oven just before draining the potatoes (next stage).

Halve and quarter the potatoes, depending on their size. Bring a medium-sized pot of water to the boil. When the water boils, add a palmful of sea salt then add the potatoes. Cook for 10 minutes. Drain the potatoes.

Put the potatoes onto the now-hot oven tray. Stir the potatoes into the oil and put in the oven for 40 to 45 minutes until a golden crust is formed on the skins.

Versatility
For another version of this classic recipe, peel the potatoes and leave them whole. Bring a pan of water to the boil. When it boils, add a palmful of sea salt, then add the potatoes. Cook for 10 minutes, then drain. Put the potatoes into the hot olive oil in the oven tray. Stir them into the oil, then put in the oven for 40 to 45 minutes, until a golden crust forms on the outside and they are soft inside. During baking, spoon oil onto the potatoes a couple of times and turn them so that an even crust forms on both sides. Turn the oven off, but leave the potatoes in to rest for another 15 minutes. Sprinkle with coarse sea salt, to taste.

Songino
Lamb's Lettuce

What you need
300 g / 10½ oz lamb's lettuce / corn salad / valerian (*valeriana*)
60 ml / 2 fl oz / 4 tbsp extra-virgin olive oil
a pinch of salt
balsamic vinegar glaze, to taste

How you make it
Wash and pat dry the lamb's lettuce. Place in a serving bowl. Add a pinch of salt, the olive oil and the balsamic vinegar glaze to taste. Mix well before serving.

Versatility
I use fig balsamic vinegar glaze, which is very sweet. It is not the easiest to find, though: try Italian delis, high-end food halls or ask a friend to bring it over for you from Italy! Otherwise, aged balsamic vinegar is a good alternative.

Pastiera Napoletana

Neapolitan Easter Cake

This cake is the epitome of celebration! It is big, rich, sweet, aromatic, filling – yet one slice is never enough. I had the good fortune of tasting a real *pastiera* made by a *bona fide* Neapolitan lady, Anna Pisa. When Easter comes, 'La Signora Anna', as she is affectionately known, fills the homes and hearts of friends, family, work colleagues and neighbours all over Milan – her adopted city – with her homemade *pastiera* as an Easter gift. The recipe, below, may seem a bit laborious, but this cake is well worth the effort!

Suitable for adults and children
Preparation time: 1 hour
Cooking time: 1 hour
Serves 10 people (if you make one large *pastiera*; or you could make two medium-sized *pastieras*, one to treat yourself and immediate family and the other to surprise your loved ones!)

What you need

For the filling:
500 g / 17½ oz *grano cotto* (ready-to-use cooked grain
    (wheat) sold in jars or tins / cans)
300 ml / 10 fl oz / 1¼ US cups milk, cold
50 g / 1¾ oz / ½ stick butter
1 fresh lemon, peel / zest of
1 fresh orange, peel / zest of
7 eggs
3 egg yolks
700 g / 1½ lb / 3 US cups granulated / white sugar
700 g / 24¾ oz ricotta cheese
50 g / 1¾ fl oz / ¼ US cup orange blossom water (one vial)
1 tsp vanilla essence
100 g / 3½ oz citron peel / candied peel
    (or substitute with dried citrus fruit pieces)
150 g / 5¼ oz / 1¼ US cup icing / confectioner's sugar,
    to dust

For the shortcrust / short / sweetcrust pastry:
500 g / 17½ oz / 4 US cups white plain / all-purpose flour
200 g / 7 oz / 1¾ sticks butter, diced
200 g / 7 oz / 1 US cup granulated / white sugar
3 eggs
1 fresh lemon, grated peel of
a pinch of salt

How you make it

In a large saucepan, place the *grano cotto* with the cold milk, constantly stirring until the mixture is creamy. Add 50 g of butter, the peel of a lemon and the peel of an orange. Put on a low heat and cook for 10 minutes, stirring until the mixture is smooth and creamy.

Turn the heat off, pour the creamy mixture into a large mixing bowl and leave it to cool down.

Using another large mixing bowl, beat the eggs and the egg yolks. Add the beaten eggs to the creamy mixture one spoon at a time.

Add the sugar and stir well. Add the ricotta and stir well. Add the orange blossom water and stir well. Add the vanilla essence and stir well. Add the citron peel and stir well.

Leave the creamy mixture to rest.

Pre-heat the oven at 180°C / 350°F / Gas Mark 4.

Make the pastry. Sift the flour onto a cold surface (marble / steel or a very large glass bowl). Dice the butter and add to the centre of the flour. Add the sugar, the eggs, the grated lemon peel and a pinch of salt.

Rinse your hands in cold water and pat dry. It is important that the pastry is not in contact with warm hands. Work all the ingredients, quickly forming a ball of dough. Wrap it in cling film / plastic wrap and leave it to rest in the fridge for 30 minutes.

Take the pastry out of the fridge and roll out with a rolling pin.

Grease, with butter, a large baking tin, 3 cm (1¼ in) deep. Lay the pastry on and pour the mixture to the brim.

With the rest of the pastry, cut long strips and lay them criss-crossed over the top.

Bake for 1 hour.

Take out of the oven, leave it to cool and dust with icing / confectioner's sugar before serving.

Avventurosi

7

Adventurous recipes

In this chapter I have selected recipes made using more 'adventurous' ingredients, not all of which may be familiar, but, to stimulate your appetite and your curiosity, I can assure you that, although the flavours are distinctive, they are well balanced, not too strong, not too spicy and not *too* peculiar...

Some recipes may look difficult, some dishes may seem strange, some ingredients may be a little difficult to source... reach beyond all this, however, and let your spirit of adventure prevail! You may be rewarded by the discovery of an unexpected, extraordinary flavour combination, or perhaps simply confirm that a particular ingredient or preparation is not for you, but you will certainly never know unless you add a little adventure to your culinary journey!

Insalata di Polpo

Octopus Salad

Oscar – whom you have already met in Chapter 2 and will encounter again in the Epilogue – is one of my food heroes, not least as he actually adores octopus. To the other children's dismay and delight, Oscar is not at all squeamish and will happily fish for an octopus, touch it and, perhaps most daringly, thoroughly enjoy eating it!

Octopus is a typical Mediterranean dish. You will find it not only in Italy but also in Greece, Spain and Portugal. In Italy, many restaurants display *insalata di polpo* on their *antipasti* counter, and, less commonly, octopus can be stewed and eaten warm with tomatoes and potatoes. I agree with Oscar, though: the salad version is my favourite, too. Eaten at room temperature, it is an all year round dish and can be served both as a starter or as part of a buffet.

If using fresh octopus, ask your fishmonger to clean it for you. Frozen octopus generally comes already cleaned and ready to cook.

Suitable for adults and adventurous children
Preparation time: 15 minutes
Cooking time: 1 hour
Serves 6 people

What you need
5 litres / 169 fl oz / 21 US cups water
1 medium (approximately 1½ kg / 3 lb 5 oz) octopus
    (sustainably sourced)

For the cooking stock:
700 ml / 23½ fl oz / 3 US cups water
700 ml / 23½ fl oz / 3 US cups extra-virgin olive oil
40 ml / 1⅓ fl oz / ⅛ US cup red wine vinegar
10 cloves garlic, peeled and whole
24 black peppercorns, whole
1 big bunch fresh flat-leaf parsley, roughly chopped
1 dry chilli pepper, roughly chopped
½ lemon, juice of

For the dressing:
50 ml / 1¾ fl oz / 3¼ tbsp extra-virgin olive oil
1 tbsp flat-leaf parsley, finely chopped
1 garlic clove, peeled and finely chopped
½ lemon, juice of
black pepper, freshly ground
a pinch of ground chilli pepper

Optional:
salt, to taste (octopus is naturally salty, so taste the dish before
    adding salt seasoning)

How you make it
Bring a large pot of unsalted water to the boil. Meanwhile, wash the octopus in cold running water.

Dip the octopus in the boiling water for 1 minute then drain in a colander. Leave the octopus to one side.

In another large pot, add all of the cooking stock ingredients and place on a low heat. Put the octopus in the stock and simmer on a low heat for approximately 1 hour, until tender.

Once cooked, leave the octopus in the stock to cool down at room temperature.

To serve, cut the octopus into small pieces. Place in a large bowl. Add all the ingredients for the dressing and serve at room temperature.

Vitel Toné

Veal with Tuna Sauce

Vitel toné (also known as *vitello tonnato*) is a typical dish from the towns of Cuneo and Alba in the region of Piedmont, northern Italy. It dates back to the 18th century and it is still a traditional favourite.

It is also a very versatile dish as it can be served either as an *antipasto* (starter) or as part of a buffet. Accompanied by a mixed salad, it can be a *secondo* (main course), too, whether eaten in a bar in, say, Milan or Turin during lunch break or prepared at home for Sunday lunch in the summer.

The sauce is made mainly with tuna and it has a salty taste that appeals to children. Use high-quality tuna fillets preserved in extra-virgin olive oil for the best taste. The look of the dish reminds me a bit of curry – not the most photogenic of meals, but certainly one of the most flavourful. Shut your eyes and savour it, you will be pleasantly surprised!

Suitable for adults and adventurous children
Preparation time: 30 minutes
Cooking time: 1½ hours
Serves 6 people

What you need
600 g / 1 lb 5 oz high-welfare veal, fillet
1 carrot
1 medium onion
1 celery stick
1 small bunch flat-leaf parsley, roughly chopped
3 bay leaves
4 cloves
4 black peppercorns
50 cl (500 ml) / 17 fl oz dry white wine
1½ litres / 51 fl oz / 6⅓ US cups water
4 eggs, hard-boiled and peeled

6 fillets of anchovies in extra-virgin olive oil
200 g / 7 oz tuna (sustainably sourced), tinned / canned or preserved in a glass jar in extra-virgin olive oil
1 tsp vinegar
60 ml / 2 fl oz / 4 tbsp extra-virgin olive oil
30 g / 1 oz salted capers, washed and de-salted
a few drops of lemon juice

How you make it
Put the veal, carrot, onion, celery, parsley, bay leaves, cloves and black pepper in a tall and narrow saucepan.

Pour the white wine over and top up with the water. Bring to the boil on a medium heat. Once boiling, lower the heat and simmer for 1½ hours.

In the meantime, boil the 4 eggs. Once cooked and cooled, peel the eggs. Put them, the anchovies, the well-drained tuna, the vinegar, the olive oil, two-thirds of the washed and desalted capers and a few drops of lemon juice in a food processor and whizz at medium speed to obtain a smooth cream. Use some of the meat stock to make the cream more fluid, as necessary, by adding a third of a glass at a time. Make sure the cream does not become too liquid, though.

Once the meat is cooked, let it cool down and then slice it in thin slices (3 to 4 mm / ⅛ in).

Lay the meat on serving plates and pour the cream over the top of each portion. Put the remaining washed and desalted capers on top of the cream to decorate.

Seppie Colorate in Umido

Colourful Cuttlefish Stew

Cuttlefish can be easily disguised and made fun for children when cut into circles. As this fish does not have a very strong 'fishy' flavour, it often appeals to younger palates especially if accompanied by the vegetables most favoured among children: peas and potatoes. The colourful yellow appearance given to this dish by the saffron may make your little ones less suspicious, more curious and ready to try something new. Similarly, if an adult you know hasn't quite grown out of their suspicion of unusual foodstuffs, give this recipe a try as the mixture of herbs, spices and seeds should soon conquer their taste-buds.

If you can't find cuttlefish at your fishmonger, substitute it with squid. Also, for this dish, I have avoided keeping and cooking the tentacles of the cuttlefish, even though these are succulent and very tasty, in order that no-one is put off from trying the recipe. Once everyone is feeling even more adventurous, though, try it with the tentacles too; remember to cook the stew for longer, up to 1 hour, as the tentacles are much harder than the rest of the cuttlefish.

Suitable for adults and adventurous children
Preparation time: 15 minutes
Cooking time: 45 minutes
Serves 6 people

What you need

4 medium cuttlefish (approximately 600 g / 1 lb 5 oz), cleaned and cut into rings (ask your fishmonger to do this for you)
100 g / 3½ oz / ⅘ US cup white plain / all-purpose flour
1 medium onion, peeled and chopped
2–3 cloves garlic (according to taste), peeled and chopped
½ small bunch fresh flat-leaf parsley, chopped
1 large potato
1 fennel bulb
60 ml / 2 fl oz / 4 tbsp extra-virgin olive oil
1 tsp dry Italian mixed herbs for fish
1 tsp fennel seeds
5 black peppercorns

1 tin / can organic chickpeas / garbanzo beans, drained (or 200 g / 7 oz dry organic chickpeas / garbanzo beans)
12 cl (120 ml) / 4 fl oz / 8 tbsp dry white wine
250 ml / 8½ fl oz / 1 US cup water
200 g / 7 oz peas
1 tsp saffron pistils (or 2 small sachets of saffron powder)
a pinch of salt

Optional (suitable for adults):
½ fresh chilli pepper, finely chopped

How you make it

Wash and pat dry the cuttlefish rings. Coat the rings with flour and put to one side.

Chop the onion, the garlic and the parsley and set to one side.

Peel the potato, cut into cubes and set one side. Peel off the outer leaves of the fennel bulb. Slice the fennel and set to one side.

Put the chopped onion, garlic and parsley into a saucepan (a clay one is best, if you have one), add the olive oil, herbs, fennel seeds and peppercorns and lightly fry for 3 minutes on a low heat.

Add the cuttlefish, the potatoes, the fennel and the chickpeas and gently simmer stirring for 5 minutes. Pour in the white wine and the water and simmer for 30 to 35 minutes, until the cuttlefish is tender.

Add the peas, the salt and the saffron and simmer for another 5 minutes. Add the chopped chilli if desired.

Serve hot.

Versatility

If you want to use dry chickpeas instead of canned, remember to soak them overnight before cooking them. Cook the chickpeas / garbanzo beans in unsalted water (three times the quantity of the pulses) for 40 minutes, until they are soft but retaining their texture. Drain and use as advised above.

Passatelli

Passatelli

This egg-and-lemon delicacy from central Italy is one of my favourite *primi*. The zest of the lemon gives freshness to the dish, which can be prepared for both winter and late summer dinners. I have included two versions: one with vegetable stock, which is much loved by the whole family, and the other with mushroom sauce and generally preferred by adults, even though I know some adventurous children who adore mushrooms. My version of *Passatelli con sugo di funghi* is inspired by the way my Italian friend chef Mauro Lucarelli makes his passatelli dough. He is truly a *maestro*!

Passatelli dough is easy to prepare, but you will require a pair of strong arms both to work the dough and to press it through the ricer or strainer! Indeed, it is usual in Italian families to ask 'the man of the house' to press the passatelli through the ricer – and you can use a food processor with the dough-mixing tool to combine the dough.

Another variable to watch out for with this recipe is breadcrumbs. Homemade breadcrumbs or those bought from your bakery or bakery section of your store have a different consistency to those that have been industrially prepared. The latter tend to be very fine in consistency and do not combine as well as the homemade ones. So, either buy them from the bakery or, if you have time and some spare stale bread, make them yourself. If you opt for using stale bread, let it dry out completely until it becomes rock hard. Then, using a food processor (blade tool) or an electric cheese grater, if you have one, finely 'grate' the dry bread and store it in an airtight glass jar, away from sunlight. It keeps for months and it can be used for many other recipes.

Also, because the breadcrumbs and cheese consistency and texture may vary, I have here added flour as an optional ingredient to the traditional recipe to help to combine the dough if required. So, if you sense that the dough is too soft, you can try adding a measure of flour accordingly. Conversely, if the dough comes up incredibly hard, add an egg to it. Indeed, the final result does also depend on the size of the eggs used in the first place. Enjoy experimenting with these variables and you, too, will master passatelli in no time!

The good news is that passatelli is cooked directly in the stock and can be served in it as soup, so… passatelli does not overcook! Additionally, because this recipe is quite unusual, you will impress your guests with something new at a dinner party.

Further good news for 'busy bees' is that passatelli can be frozen and cooked at different times. Once you have made the dough, press it through the ricer and lay the resulting passatelli on a plastic tray or serving plate, making sure not to squash them together, then put them in the freezer for a few hours. Once frozen, put them in a container suitable for freezers and store up to one month. When you want to use the passatelli, take them out of the freezer and immediately cook from frozen, plunging them into the hot stock as per the original recipe.

Suitable for children and adults
Preparation time: 15 minutes (plus 30 minutes of 'rest' time)
Cooking time: 10 minutes
Serves 6–8 people

What you need
6 large eggs
300 g / 10½ oz / 2½ US cups breadcrumbs, dry
200 g / 7⅛ oz / 1 US cup parmesan, grated
a generous pinch of ground nutmeg
a generous pinch of freshly ground black pepper
a pinch of salt

Optional:
70 g / 7 tbsp white plain / all-purpose flour
    (use if consistency of dough is too soft and sticky)
1 lemon, zest of (not to be used when making *Passatelli con sugo di funghi*)

How you make it
In a large mixing bowl, beat the eggs. Combine the breadcrumbs and the parmesan and mix well.

Add flour to the dough as required, according to its consistency. Do not over do it, though, or the dough may become too hard once it has been left to rest and so particularly difficult to press through the ricer!

Grate the lemon peel and add this zest to the mixture (if you are making *Passatelli in brodo*; omit this ingredient for the *Passatelli con sugo di funghi*). Finally, add the nutmeg, the pepper and the salt.

Work the mixture, which, at the beginning, will be sticky and then crumbly. Keep working with your hands until you obtain a solid dough. Wrap the dough in a plastic food bag, cling film / plastic wrap or put it in Tupperware container to rest. Leave it to rest in the fridge for 30 minutes, checking that the dough does not crumble when handled.

Use a passatelli ricer or, if you do not have one, a potato ricer with 6 mm / ¼ in holes. (It is well worth investing in a ricer as it can be used to make mashed potatoes and gnocchi as well as passatelli.)

Standing with caution by the saucepan of boiling stock (*Passatelli in brodo* recipe, following), put a small amount of dough at a time into the ricer and firmly press it through directly into the stock. A kind of thick 'spaghetti' will come through the ricer; with the help of a knife, cut the passatelli to 4-cm (1½-in) long pieces. Once in the boiling vegetable stock, the passatelli will be cooked in 7 to 10 minutes.

Versatility
If you need to vary the quantities – e.g., if you want to make one big batch, freeze it and then use when needed, or if you want to make them fresh each time – here are the per-person measures for each ingredient:

1 large egg
50 g / 1¾ oz / ½ US cup breadcrumbs, dry
30 g / 1 oz / 2½ tbsp parmesan, grated
a pinch of ground nutmeg
a smidgeon of freshly ground black pepper
a smidgeon of salt

Optional:
up to 10 g / 1 tbsp white plain / all-purpose flour
⅙ lemon, zest of

Passatelli in Brodo

Passatelli in Vegetable Stock

Suitable for children and adults
Preparation time: 10 minutes (for the stock)
Cooking time: 30 minutes

What you need
1 large onion, peeled
1 large celery stick, trimmed
1 large carrot, peeled
1 large potato, peeled
1 leek, trimmed
1 fennel bulb (when in season), trimmed
2 sprigs fresh thyme, finely chopped
½ bunch flat-leaf parsley, finely chopped
a pinch of salt
30 ml / 1 fl oz / 2 tbsp extra-virgin olive oil
2 litres / 68 fl oz / 8¼ US cups water

Optional (to decorate):
parmesan, freshly grated
extra-virgin olive oil
lemon juice, freshly squeezed
black pepper, freshly ground
chilli pepper flakes, to taste

How you make it

Peel the vegetables. Put them, all the other ingredients and the water into a tall pan. Put on a high heat and cover with a lid. Bring to the boil, turn the heat down to low and let the stock boil for a further 20 minutes.

After this time, take the vegetables out and leave the stock on the heat. Place the passatelli in the boiling stock to cook for 7 to 10 minutes. You will notice that the passatelli will rise to the surface after a few minutes – they are almost ready. Scoop the passatelli out with the stock ready to be served.

Sprinkle some freshly grated parmesan cheese, drizzle some extra-virgin olive oil, squeeze a couple of drops of lemon juice, grind black pepper and add a little chilli pepper to your taste before serving.

Serve hot as a soup.

Versatility

Passatelli also marry very well with chicken stock. Indeed, traditionally they are cooked in either chicken or beef stock. Just add a whole chicken or chicken legs to your vegetable stock ingredients above and cook slowly for 1½ hours, until the meat is cooked. Take out the chicken and the vegetables and then filter to obtain a clear stock in which to cook the passatelli.

Passatelli con Sugo di Funghi

Passatelli with Mushroom Sauce

Suitable for adults and adventurous children
Preparation time: 15 minutes (for the mushroom sauce)
Cooking time: 20 minutes

What you need

400 g / 14 oz / 7½ US cups mixed variety, fresh mushrooms
    (use a variety of fresh mushrooms for different flavours
    and textures; or, choose the best and use porcini /
    cep mushrooms!)
2–3 cloves of garlic (according to taste),
    peeled and finely sliced
½ bunch flat-leaf parsley, finely chopped
45 ml / 1½ fl oz / 3 tbsp extra-virgin olive oil
15 cl (150 ml) / 5 fl oz dry white wine
a pinch of salt
black pepper, freshly ground

How you make it

Clean the mushrooms by brushing them, especially the underside, to eliminate any dirt. Peel and finely slice the garlic. Wash and finely chop the parsley.

Into a large saucepan, pour the extra-virgin olive oil. Add the garlic and put on a low heat for a few minutes, making sure the garlic does not burn. When the oil is hot, add the mushrooms and half of the parsley. Stir and cook for a few minutes, turning the heat up to medium. Add the wine and let it evaporate for a few minutes. Turn the heat back down to low and gently cook until the juice has evaporated and the mushrooms have reduced in size.

Prepare and cook the passatelli as per the recipe on page 231, but remember not to use the grated lemon peel for this dish. Also, if you feel you need to add a little flour to help the pasta dough ingredients combine, don't add any more than a maximum of 2 tbsp as the dough will firm up more once it has been left to rest.

Once cooked, drain the passatelli from the stock. Place on a serving plate or in individual pasta bowls and add the mushroom sauce.

Sprinkle some fresh parsley on top and add freshly ground black pepper if desired.

Serve hot.

Polenta e Funghi

Polenta and Mushrooms

This is a wonderful warming dish for the first of the cold autumnal days. I have included it in the 'adventurous' chapter because mushrooms seem to be something of a contentious ingredient: people either love them or hate them, particularly their texture. If you are a mushroom lover, like me, choose your favourite mushrooms of your choice, from the most common closed-cup or button mushroom to chestnut, cremini, girolle / chanterelles or the finest porcini.

Polenta has such a mild taste that is almost impossible not to like it and it is an excellent accompaniment when enhanced by other flavours. If mushrooms are definitively not your favourite ingredient, though, try polenta with melted Gorgonzola, Fontina or Taleggio cheese on top, sprinkled with walnut pieces / kernels. Once you have put all the ingredients together, grill for a couple of minutes and enjoy it with a fine glass of red wine. You can opt to melt the three cheeses together for a richer flavour.

Suitable for adults and adventurous children
Preparation time: 15 minutes
Cooking time: 60 minutes
Serves 4 people

What you need
For the polenta:
1¾ litres / 44 fl oz / 5½ US cups water
400 g / 14 oz polenta *fioretto* (corn flour, fine mill variety)
1 tbsp (heaped) coarse sea salt

For the mushroom sauce:
500 g / 17½ oz mushrooms (choose your favourite(s))
2 cloves of garlic, peeled and crushed
1 bunch flat-leaf parsley, finely chopped
200 g / 7 oz / 1¾ sticks butter
a pinch of salt
10 g / ⅓ oz / 1 tbsp potato flour
25 cl (250 ml) / 8½ fl oz dry white wine
black pepper, freshly ground

How you make it
For the polenta:
Bring a large saucepan of water to the boil. Add the sea salt. Lower the heat to the minimum.

Pour the polenta into the water, a little bit at a time, stirring constantly with a wooden spoon.

Keep stirring constantly, making sure that lumps do not form. Because of its fine mill, the *fioretto* Polenta stays soft.

Turn the heat off and leave the polenta in the saucepan to set for a few minutes.

For the mushroom sauce:
Clean the mushrooms. Slice them and set to one side. Crush the garlic and finely chop the parsley.

In a large frying pan (with a lid, used later), melt the butter and put it on a low heat. Add the garlic and the salt. Stirring constantly, add the potato flour, a little bit at a time, making sure the mixture does not become lumpy. Add the mushrooms and half of the parsley. Stir for a few minutes.

Pour the white wine over the mushrooms and let it evaporate for a few minutes. Stir well. Simmer for 10 minutes until some of the juice has thickened and the mushrooms are soft. Turn the heat off and keep the mushroom sauce warm in the pan, covered with a lid.

Dish the polenta out on a large serving plate and present the sauce at the side.

Versatility
If you do not have an hour to make polenta, pre-cooked polenta is also widely available and takes between 15 and 30 minutes to make, depending on the brand.

Verdure Ripiene

Stuffed Vegetables

This is an extremely 'versatile' vegetable dish, in that it can be a starter or a main course, served as part of a buffet or at a barbeque, and prepared as a vegetarian or a non-vegetarian recipe. Your choice of vegetables can be adapted, too, in line with seasonal availability.

Suitable for adults and adventurous children
Preparation time: 15 minutes
Cooking time: 40 minutes
Serves 4 people

What you need
For the meat version:
1 egg
200 g / 7 oz extra-lean minced / ground meat
    (beef or pork, as preferred)
100 g / 4 oz *prosciutto cotto*
    (or substitute with honey-roasted ham)
50 g / 1¾ oz Fontina cheese (medium and tasty) or Taleggio
    cheese (soft and full flavour) or mozzarella cheese (soft
    and very mild), diced
50 g / 1¾ oz Quark cheese
1 bunch fresh flat-leaf parsley, finely chopped
1 tsp Italian dry mixed herbs
salt
black pepper, freshly ground
vegetables (of your choice, e.g. 1 aubergine, 1 courgette /
    zucchini, 1 tomato, 1 pepper, 1 artichoke, etc.;
    or, you may prefer to use only, e.g. tomatoes)
50 g / 1¾ oz / ½ US cup breadcrumbs, dry

For the vegetarian version:
Use the same ingredients as above except the meat (mince, ham) and check that the cheeses use non-animal rennet. Use 5 egg whites, beaten, and 2 egg yolks, beaten.

How you make it
Pre-heat the oven to 180°C / 350°F / Gas Mark 4.

Beat the eggs well. Add the mince and ham (if used), cheeses, parsley, dry herbs, salt and ground pepper.

To fill the courgette / zucchini, pepper and aubergine / eggplant:
Halve the courgette / zucchini, pepper and aubergine / eggplant. Scoop out the flesh. Fill with the mixture and top with breadcrumbs.

To fill the artichoke:
Remove the outer leaves until you reach the 'heart' of the artichoke where the lighter coloured, more tender leaves are. To open up the artichoke, beat it on a hard surface. Sprinkle it with water until the leaves are moist. Fill it with the mixture. Top with breadcrumbs.

To fill the tomato:
Take the top side of the tomato off by slicing it. Scoop out the pulp. Fill the tomato with the mixture. Top up with breadcrumbs.

Now, place the vegetables of your choice in a deep oven tray (lined with baking paper / parchment) with 1 cm (⅓ in) of water and bake for 40 minutes.

Tutti cuochi

Little cooks, big cooks

Through this chapter I hope to share the great fun I had with the children when we cooked together. I also want to pass on the enjoyment I experienced, as a child, of creating similar dishes with my mother. We spent countless contented days making gnocchi and grape jam, for example, and these memories remain vivid. Recipes for both feature in this chapter.

Banana and chocolate gelato, also included in this chapter, are more 'moments' lived with my own children, and everything blurs into a magical vision where I find myself, with a furtive glance, licking the last spoonful of cream off the bowl and being 'told off' by my own girls for being greedy!

It was in honour of experiences such as these that I decided to found the Gnocchi Fan Club. I put my white cooking dress on and off I went to get everything organized. I made gnocchi, offered them to children who had never tried them before and successfully had them join the Club. I made gnocchi with the eight children who have been named elsewhere as Stars of the Book and we not only had great fun, but we also indulged in tasting the gnocchi topped with all three of the sauces featured in this book! These children are certainly part of the Club – and several adults have since joined too....

Homemade potato gnocchi are simply sublime. 'Simply' because they are made using basic, natural ingredients – potatoes, flour and salt – and 'sublime' because their soft, smooth texture enveloped by a succulent sauce delicately titillates the taste-buds. I know that there are people who have tried only commercially produced gnocchi sold in supermarkets and found them 'simply revolting' and I cannot agree more. These are often made with semolina, not real potatoes. Make them yourselves and discover the real taste! If you love potatoes, you will love gnocchi.

These little Italian dumplings bring joy to the table. Historically, in the countryside of the Emilia-Romagna region, gnocchi were made to celebrate the safe birth of a baby boy in the family. Similarly, a baby girl would be welcomed by a sizeable, succulent serving of *lasagna*.[1]

1   Dickie, J. (2008) *Delizia! The epic history of the Italians and their food*. New York: Free Press.

Gnocchi

Gnocchi

Enjoy the ritual of making fresh pasta at home, shaping these mini masterpieces with your own hands and sharing the pleasure of eating them among good company.

I suggest that you keep the following quantities as a base with which to easily work the gnocchi dough a little at a time. Double the quantities if you are making gnocchi for a party of 10 to 12 people, but do still combine the ingredients in two batches, as this will make the work so much easier! Gnocchi can also be frozen, so once you have made a good quantity, you can enjoy them for several meals. Simply cook them from frozen.

Suitable for adults and children
Preparation time: 30 minutes
Cooking time: 40 minutes
Serves 4–6 people

What you need
1 kg / 2½ lb Désirée potatoes (or substitute with Russet, Nicola or another floury, but not waxy, variety)
3½ litres / 118 fl oz / 14¾ US cups water (for the potatoes)
10 g / ½ tbsp / a palmful coarse sea salt
200 g / 7 oz / 1½ US cups *farina* / flour for making pasta (type 00, *dopio zero*) (or substitute with plain / all-purpose white flour), plus extra for dusting
1 egg, room temperature
3½ litres / 118 fl oz / 14¾ US cups water (for the gnocchi)

How you make it
Wash the potatoes. Put them, whole and unpeeled, into a large saucepan filled with cold salted water. Boil the potatoes for about 30 to 35 minutes until soft. Drain and peel the potatoes while they are still hot. Immediately push through a potato ricer (or food mill) onto a floured flat surface, forming a mound. Allow to cool to room temperature.

Sift half of the flour on top of the potato mound and make a well in the centre.

Lightly beat the egg and add.

Use your hands to mix and form a smooth, elastic and soft dough. While making the dough, add the rest of the flour gradually, keeping a couple of handfuls to one side to roll out the dough later on. Work the dough quickly for a short period, as overworking it will make the gnocchi too heavy. Keep in mind the ratio of flour to potato: too much flour will make the gnocchi hard, while too much potato means the gnocchi will dissolve whilst cooking.

Leave the dough to rest for 5 minutes while you clean the surface on which you will cut and shape the gnocchi.

Take two trays or large serving plates and sprinkle with flour. The gnocchi will be placed on these before being boiled.

Once the surface is clean and dry, split the dough into two parts. Sprinkle some flour on the surface and roll one of the two parts of dough into a long sausage approximately 1½ cm (½ in) thick.

Cut the sausage into small pieces, approximately 1 cm (⅓ in) each.

Using a fork, put one of the small pieces of dough on the prongs and, lightly pressing with your thumb, roll the *gnocco* off the fork. Repeat for all pieces.

This process will give the gnocchi the perfect ridged texture to better absorb the sauce. If you wish, you can avoid this stage, though, and only have gnocchi cut into small pieces with a smooth surface.

Bring a large saucepan of water to the boil. When the water boils, add salt. Put no more than 15 gnocchi at a time into the boiling water; cook for about 2 to 3 minutes. When the gnocchi rise to the surface, they are cooked. Scoop the gnocchi out with a strainer. Put them into bowls and serve with the chosen sauce (a few suggested recipes for which follow this one). Adjust the quantities according to the number of people you are cooking for.

Salsa di Pomodoro
Tomato Sauce

What you need
1 onion, finely chopped
1–2 garlic cloves, finely chopped
60 ml / 2 fl oz / 4 tbsp extra-virgin olive oil
tomato passata
a pinch of salt

Optional:
parmesan, grated
black pepper, freshly ground

How you make it
Finely chop the onion and the garlic. Put the olive oil, the onion and the garlic into a casserole and gently cook on a low heat until the onion is soft. Add the tomato passata and a pinch of salt. Simmer for 20 minutes. Add the sauce to the gnocchi and top with parmesan cheese and black pepper, if desired.

Crema di Gorgonzola
Gorgonzola Sauce

What you need
1 tbsp butter, softened
a pinch of nutmeg
a pinch of salt
black pepper, freshly ground
1 medium slice creamy Gorgonzola
parmesan, to decorate

How you make it
In a saucepan, melt a small quantity of butter on a low heat. Add the nutmeg, salt and pepper. Add the cheese and let it melt. Serve the sauce on the gnocchi and garnish with a little parmesan.

Pesto
Pesto Sauce

What you need
a handful pine nuts (approximately 30 g / 1 oz), toasted
1 bunch fresh basil (approximately 100 g / 3½ oz), washed
½–2 garlic clove(s) (to taste / if cooking for young children),
    crushed
a pinch of salt
75–90 ml / 2½–3 fl oz / 5–6 tbsp extra-virgin olive oil,
    plus some to drizzle
100 g / 3½ oz / 1 US cup parmesan cheese (or, for a richer
    taste, 50 g / 1¾ oz / ½ US cup grated Parmigiano-
    Reggiano and 50 g mature Pecorino Sardo), grated
a pinch of nutmeg, freshly ground
black pepper, freshly ground

How you make it
Prepare all the ingredients before you start making the pesto
in the mortar.

Put a frying pan on a high heat. Put in the pine nuts. Take
the pan away from the heat and, moving the pan in circular
movements, toast the pine nuts for a few minutes until
they colour.

Wash the basil leaves in cold water. Put the basil, the garlic
and the salt in a mortar and gently grind into a paste with the
pestle adding a little olive oil. Add the pine nuts, the cheese
and the nutmeg to the paste and grind with the pestle. Place
the paste in a bowl, add the pepper and the rest of the olive

oil and mix well until the paste becomes smoother. If you
don't have pestle and mortar, put the ingredients except the
olive oil in a food processor and gently whizz on a low speed.
Drizzle the olive oil in a little at a time while whizzing the
other ingredients.

Add the pesto to the gnocchi with a generous amount of
grated parmesan cheese and a little drizzle of extra virgin
olive oil over the top. Add freshly ground black pepper
if desired.

If you make pesto without garlic, you will have a delicate basil
sauce, which may please the palate of young children and
those who are not keen on garlic as a flavour.

Making Jam

Making jam is easy, fun and good for the spirit. Use whichever fruit takes your fancy. One of the following is quite an unusual jam that I always made with my mother and that now my girls make with me.

Grape jam is the jam you will be making from September until Christmas and your provision will last all year round. Use it to spread on toasted and buttered bread, to sweeten plain yogurt or to fill a jam tart. If you are adventurous enough, savour this jam with cheese and warm toasted bread.

The other recipe I am presenting is to be made in the summer and it is not strictly jam but more of a preserve. An exquisite jar of yellow peaches in syrup. July and beginning of August are the best months to preserve peaches. Choose firm peaches that haven't fully ripened yet.

To successfully preserve, it is very important that the jars are thoroughly cleaned. Wash the recycled jars and tops with hot salted water and a drop of lemon. Rinse well with hot water. Lay washed clean kitchen towels on a table and place the jars and the tops upside down to dry. This process is free from chemical detergents, good for your health and the environment.

Once the jars and tops are cleaned, you can sterilize them. There are two methods. After having washed the jar and top, place them upside down in a large and tall saucepan lined with kitchen towels and boil for 30 minutes. Using tongs take them out of the boiling water and dry them upside down on washed clean kitchen towels. The other way to sterilize is to place the closed jars full of goodies in a large and tall saucepan lined with tea towels and filled with water boiling for 30 minutes.

Use 250–500 g (300–600 ml / 10½–21 fl oz) capacity jars so that, once opened, the content can be quickly consumed. Once the jars have been opened, store them in the fridge and eat the contents within a week.

Winter

Marmellata di Uva
Grape Jam

What you need
2 kg / 4 lb 6 oz white grapes
1 lemon, juice of
500 g / 17½ oz / 2½ US cups granulated / white sugar

How you make it
Put the grapes, lemon juice and sugar into a large saucepan on a low to medium heat.

Gently stir with a wooden spoon and bring to the boil. When the skin and the pips of the grapes come to the surface, gently scoop them out using a strainer. Keep stirring gently to reduce the amount of froth forming during cooking.

Let the jam cook on a low heat for approximately 1 hour and 15 minutes until it starts to stick to the wooden spoon. The longer the jam cooks, the more it will set – although grape jam tends to be quite runny.

Pour the jam hot into clean, sterilized glass jars. Close with airtight / hermetically sealed tops and let them rest upside down until cold.

Summer

Squisite Pesche Sotto Vetro
An Exquisite Jar of Peaches

What you need
2 kg / 4 lb 6 oz peaches (yellow flesh)
300 g / 10½ oz / 1½ US cups granulated / white sugar
2 litres / 68 fl oz / 8½ US cups water
½ lemon, peel / zest of

How you make it
In a large saucepan make syrup by boiling the water, sugar and lemon peel together for 5 minutes. Cool down to room temperature.

Blanch the peaches for a few seconds in hot water. Then peel the peaches, halve them and remove the stone.

Place the peaches into clean glass jars. Pour the syrup into the glass jars. Close the jars tightly.

Line a large, tall saucepan with two kitchen towels so that the jars are protected during the next stage (when boiling), avoiding breakage.

Carefully place the jars in the saucepan, making sure the kitchen towels separate them, creating a buffer. Fill the saucepan with enough water to cover the jars. Put on a medium heat. When the water reaches boiling point, boil for further 30 minutes. Turn the heat off and let it cool down.

When the water and the jars are cold, dry them up thoroughly and store in a cool place away from sunlight.

Making Gelato

Italian summer = *gelato*. It is as simple as that. In my family, the two favourite *gelati* are chocolate and banana. I make *gelato* as often as possible, and so decided to buy an easy to use, economical ice cream maker. It is a small (half-litre) container that can be easily stored in the freezer, ready for whenever we fancy ice cream.

Gelato al Cioccolato
Chocolate Gelato

Chocolate gelato can be made with both dark and milk chocolate. If you are making dark chocolate gelato, use the quantity of sugar I have given here, or use a little less if you like the bitterness of the chocolate. If you are making milk chocolate gelato, use 100 g / 3½ oz / ½ US cup of sugar.

What you need
100 g / 3½ oz dark / bittersweet chocolate
   (70% cocoa solids)
200 ml / 6¾ fl oz / ¾ US cup milk
1 egg
120–150 g / 4¼–5½ oz / ½–¾ US cup demerara / raw sugar
   (according to taste)
200 g / 7 oz whipping / whipped cream (minimum 35% fat)
1 tsp vanilla essence

How you make it
Break the chocolate into small pieces and place in a heatproof bowl with 3 tablespoons of milk.

Put a saucepan half filled with water on a low heat. In it, place a waterproof bowl in which to melt the chocolate. Stir the chocolate pieces occasionally as they melt. When the chocolate has completely melted, let it cool down.

Using an electric hand-held whisk, beat the egg and the sugar together. Warm the milk up and slowly add it, stirring constantly.

Clean the electric whisk and use it to whip the cream. Remember that it is advisable to whip cream in an ice-cold steel or glass mixing bowl as, in cold conditions, the cream will whip better and more quickly.

Add the whipped cream to the egg and sugar mixture one spoonful at a time.

Fold in the melted chocolate and mix well.

Put the mixture into the ice cream maker and churn for 30 to 40 minutes (follow the manufacturer's instructions).

When ready, freeze it.

Versatility
If you store homemade ice cream for a couple of days in the freezer, before serving it, take it out of the freezer, whizz in a food processor on a low setting for a few seconds and return it to the freezer for 10 minutes. In this way, the *gelato* will regain its softness. Do not refreeze if there is any left over.

Gelato alla Banana
Banana Gelato

What you need
4 ripe bananas, mashed
1 egg
100 g / 3½ oz / ½ US cup demerara / raw sugar
200 ml / 6¾ fl oz / ¾ US cup milk
200 g / 7 oz whipping / whipped cream (minimum 35% fat)
1 tbsp acacia honey
1 tsp vanilla essence

How you make it
Mash the bananas and set to one side.

Using an electric hand-held whisk, beat the egg with the sugar. Warm the milk up and slowly add it, stirring constantly.

Clean the electric whisk then use it to whip the cream.

Remember that it is advisable to whip cream in an ice-cold steel or glass mixing bowl as, in cold conditions, the cream will whip better and more quickly.

Add the whipped cream to the egg and sugar mixture one spoonful at a time.

Add the mashed bananas, honey and vanilla essence and mix well.

Put the mixture into the ice cream maker and churn for 30 to 40 minutes (follow the manufacturer's instruction).

When ready, freeze it.

Epilogue: Stars of the book

The eight children I asked to join me in this project are the stars of the book. They all live in London, but these 'city kids' have a good grasp of the look, taste and provenance of most fruit and vegetables, and they have all been exposed to diverse cultures and developed a keen curiosity for 'unfamiliar' foods and dishes. They are living proof that a palate can be educated from an early age.

During a three-day workshop I organized with the children, we discussed their favourite foodstuffs, and their preferences varied from fish and seafood to meat, a variety of vegetables and the rich, bittersweet flavour of dark chocolate (85% cocoa). They were happy to try new dishes and, with critical observation, they selected their favourite and explained their choice. They often also encouraged each other to try food, engaging in a discussion that would have pleased any food critic.

This chain reaction had shown up before, in a gathering I organized a few months earlier. Tito and I were testing some of the 'Special occasions' (Chapter 6) recipes at my house in London and I had invited some 'little friends' to dine with my daughters in order that the recipes might be tasted by the best food critics as far as this project is concerned. The table was laid in the garden and Maddy, Célia, Oliver, Leo, Tania, Nicoletta and Sofia, aged between 7 and 12, happily sat together around it. They tried various dishes and gave scores from '1' to '10' for each dish, explaining their ratings. A discussion concerning the texture, smell, appearance and consistency of the food took place between them without being prompted by any of the adults present. I was surprised at the accuracy of the observations and by the intuitiveness of the children

with regards to ingredients distinguished through tasting the food.

Maddy and Célia had many times before eaten at our house but we never had an open discussion about the food they were served. I know for a fact that Maddy is one of those wonderful children who has a good appetite... as long as you do not give her potatoes, which apparently are 'too much of a bland taste for her'! When she was offered gnocchi, she was told that potatoes were one of the ingredients. She still tried them though and, to her surprise and my delight, she loved gnocchi with tomato sauce and pesto (*see* pages 244–247). Combining potatoes with other ingredients had helped her to overcome her resistance to this tasty tuber. She also admitted that she liked gnocchi because they were Sofia's favourite... Positive peer pressure? I will let you draw your own conclusions! Maddy's main experience of food at home is British, French and classic Italian.

Célia has been a frequent guest for breakfast, lunch and dinner for many years. Even when she was 4 years old, I always fed her everything we were having, without fussing too much if it was something with which she was not familiar. I have always said to her, 'Just try it, you may be surprised!' Célia's favourite out of all my recipes is the green vegetable soup (page 118), but, there again, we never discussed in great detail what I actually put in her favourite dish. She is very willing to try new things, though, and politely frank in her comments if she does not appreciate a

particular flavour. At home, Célia is used to French, British and Italian cuisine.

Oliver is a 'connoisseur' when it comes to food and, at the age of 12, enjoys cooking for his family. He had been our guest with his family a few times before, but we never had the chance before now to talk about food at any great length. It was at that particular dinner organized for the recipe testing that I realized he was so knowledgeable when it came to distinguishing ingredients and flavours. He has a real passion and he stimulated the other children's enthusiasm with his comments. British, French and Italian cuisines are Oliver's forté.

Leo and Tania returned to take part in the workshop for the book. Tania is very enthusiastic and quite inquisitive in her tastes. She is the eldest of the group and so has experimented more with food and developed her 'sense of adventure' towards it. Tania enjoyed learning to cook her favourite dish – pasta with Mediterranean fish (page 178) – and is now mastering it at home. She is a good influence on her younger brother Leo as she encourages him to try new foods and flavours – not an easy task!

Leo is the 'critic' of the group. Not easily impressed and not easily led either, he is quite particular about what he likes and what he doesn't. For me, he was the real challenge. I knew that his appreciation of a dish was a hard-earned compliment. Leo's tastes do not favour 'bland' or 'easy' food over more challenging or sophisticated preparations. He is, for example, a fan of guacamole. It is simply that he is very clear in his mind what kind of flavours and, especially, appearances of food he prefers.

Both Leo and Tania have a broad exposure to a wide variety of foods. They are regularly taken out to restaurants (cooking is not their mother's favourite pastime and, apart from barbequing, Dad's no master chef, either!), and, in previous chapters, I have noted the importance of doing this as an enriching experience both for an appreciation of a variety of foods and the pleasure of enjoying a meal in good company in an environment that also requires some social skills. Leo and Tania's family enjoy going to British, Indian, Mexican, Spanish, German and, of course, Italian restaurants. An established appreciation of Italian cuisine seems to be present in every child I have spoken to, irrespective of nationality, which surely bears out Beppe Severgnini's claim, noted earlier, of a worldwide passion for it!

This experience of children discussing food between themselves with such enthusiasm reinforced my idea of organizing a workshop for the book. There are many children with an enthusiastic attitude towards good food and who are open to new discoveries, just as there are many other children who need a little encouragement to embrace new adventures. One day my daughters Nicoletta and Sofia came home from school to what was for both them and me front-page news: 'Oscar eats octopus!' At the age of 9 – and well before then – Oscar, born in England and living in London, loved octopus. He not only eats octopus (*see* page 224) but tells us that he has caught it in Greece, carrying on a very old fishing tradition that requires significant skill. The photograph

on the opposite page, taken in Sicily, shows a rare depiction of fishing for octopus.

Oscar likes salty, savoury and spicy flavours. Among his favourites are anchovies, olives, tapenade, black pepper and 'smelly cheeses'. Oscar has experienced the joy of picking strawberries and raspberries and eating them, there and then, in his family's allotment. On the first day of the workshop, he was sent to the vegetable patch of our house to pick whichever vegetable he fancied. He was very comfortable with doing this and returned victorious with a beetroot, which he had recognized and chosen!

During the three days spent together, an interesting mechanism triggered between Oscar and Leo. In the kitchen, we had

two octopuses. One was for showing the children and photographing and the other for cooking. Oscar was given an octopus in a carrier bag to show to the other children. As soon as he took the octopus out of the bag, the other children fled, screaming and running as fast as they could. An unplanned and, certainly unforeseen, game had started! Oscar had great fun, especially chasing the girls!

In spite of this fun, though, Oscar was actually trying to convince the other children to stop and look at the octopus as it is quite an amazing piece of engineering created by Mother Nature. The only one who stopped to look was Leo.

Oscar taught Leo everything he knew about the octopus. He even tried to convince him that 'it is the best food ever'!

The other boy who took part in the book project was Ben. He is the youngest and was 5 years old at the time of the workshop. He is the sweetest little boy, a trait well reflected in his tastes as far as food is concerned: the sweeter and starchier, the better! Chocolate, cakes, pasta, bread and potatoes all give him great pleasure. He is also a very good fruit eater, though, being used to picking and enjoying fresh fruit at his parents' allotment. In spite of his 'sweet tooth' and his young age, Ben did really well with eating the unfamiliar foods he was offered. Once it was explained to him what the ingredients were, he happily tried everything and chose his favourites. He thoroughly enjoyed sharing the meal with the other children, showing impeccable manners and a jovial character that make him very popular among adults and children alike.

Angelica and Hester, despite being two truly English roses, are Mediterranean girls at heart. Angelica loves calamari, salt and lemon, three ingredients that together create one of the most popular

Mediterranean dishes, *Calamari alla Romana* (page 127). Angelica has quite a discerning palate that favours extremes: either savoury and sharp or sweet and almost bordering on sickly. One of her favourite cakes is lemon tart, in which she enjoys just the right balance.

Hester is in the same league as Oscar with her relatively advanced tastes. Clams are her favourite. Seafood can be quite daunting, strange-looking, a bit exotic and not always a popular choice, especially among children. However, Hester likes clams as much as she likes prawns and, thanks to her influence, Sofia tried prawns and discovered that she actually likes them too. The two friends have been seen fighting over a plate of *Fritto misto* (mixed fried fish) when only a few prawns were left! *Spaghetti con le vongole* (page 108) is the best dish one can prepare for Hester, followed by any chocolate dessert, to which she is also known to be very partial.

Nicoletta, who can eat three chocolate ice creams in three seconds, shares the same passion for chocolate as Hester and Ben. Being half Italian, she honours her origins by favouring tiramisu, chocolate ice cream and *pasta con i broccoli* (page 105). The latter she has asked me to cook many times. Nicoletta loves all vegetables, even raw onions, has a tendency towards experimentation, with one of her more unusual recipes being a 'sliced cheddar sandwich filled with marmite' in which the 'sandwich' featured no bread!

Sofia is 'Miss Fruity'. Among the youngest in the group, she, perhaps surprisingly, favours fruit over any other too 'elaborate' sweet flavour. Strawberry and banana ice cream are her favourites. It is a joy to see her reach for the fruit bowl when she fancies a snack. This does not mean that, presented with a nice big slice of cake, she would turn it down. A piece of good-quality milk chocolate always wins her over, too. It is the pureness of a flavour that seems to appeal to Sofia. *Torta di ricotta* (page 157), for example, is her favourite cake, with its delicate flavour. She loves cooking, too, and her two speciality dishes are gnocchi, which she makes and eats with equal enthusiasm and speed, and refreshing mixed salads.

Stars of the book

Insalata di Polpo
Octopus Salad

'I like all seafood… octopus looks weird, like a monster, and the first time I tried it I thought that it would taste as strange as it looks, and that I wouldn't like it, but actually it tastes fantastic. It was hard to put in my mouth because it looked so scary, and I had to really try to make myself eat it, but then I found I liked the taste. It is oily and chewy. I like the fact that when I have it in a restaurant I have something that most kids won't try. It makes me feel adventurous!'

Linguine al Pesce Mediterraneo
Linguine with Mediterranean Fish

'My favourite dish was definitely the linguine with Mediterranean fish. I absolutely loved it. The fish was delicious especially mixed together with the pasta, the tomatoes and the olives. It tasted simply amazing with that final pinch of black pepper.

This fish was fun to cook and the little effort put into preparing it, was definitely worth it because I made it for my mother and my mum enjoyed it too!'

'What do you find in your salad?'
by Sofia

Do you find a snail?

Do you find a slug?

Do you find a bug?

Do you find a ladybird as red as a cherry?

Do you find a millipede as long as a ferry?

Do you find a tarantula (really hairy!)?

Do you find a caterpillar big and green?

Do you find a worm really lean?

... But... I am not so keen ...

I wish I could have a normal salad!

Angelica

Calamari alla Romana
Fried Calamari

'I like calamari because it's chewy and crunchy. I like the flavour and the breadcrumbs around it. I love when I squeeze lemon on it because it tastes really nice.'

Ben

Budino Freddo
Cold Chocolate Budino

'I LOVE chocolate! It's sweet and it melts in my mouth... it's a treat, and when I eat it, it makes me feel happy. My favourite type of chocolate is milk chocolate and I like it best when it's in the shape of a chocolate bar, it just tastes better than chocolate buttons... I don't know why...'

Nicoletta

Orecchiette con i Broccoli
Orecchiette with Broccoli

'I love pasta with broccoli because I can't live without pasta and I love broccoli. Broccoli look like a tree. The pasta shape I like to have with broccoli is orecchiette because they are thick, a bit chewy and tasty... I always ask for seconds of pasta with broccoli... but I don't always get it!'

Sofia

Gnocchi
Gnocchi

'I like gnocchi because it is made out of potatoes and I really love potatoes! Gnocchi is a savoury dish. Making gnocchi is fun because you get all your hands sticky and you can make gnocchi with mummy or your friends. What I love the most about making gnocchi is to make the long sausage rolls. My favourite sauces to go with them are the tomato sauce and the pesto with lots and lots of parmesan cheese...'

'The Mumbly, Crumbly Meatloaf'
by Leo

The Mumbly Crumbly Meatloaf

is the crumbliest thing in the world.

But, because the Mumbly Crumbly Meatloaf

keeps getting eaten,

the Mumbly Crumbly Meatloaf

is always very sad

Polpettone
Meatloaf

'Meatloaf is a lovely kind of food! It has meat on the outside and on the inside there's spinach, egg and other delicious things. I would give 9.9 out of 10 stars. I love it because it's meatish and is soft and easy to bite.'

Spaghetti con le Vongole
Spaghetti with Clams

'I love *spaghetti vongole* because of the yummy taste. Spaghetti is my favourite food. I like the little clams because it is fun getting them out of their shells.'

Select bibliography

ADNKronos (2011) 'Nelle grandi città i cittadini coltivano sui tetti!', *L'Aromatario*, Winter 2011, numero 6: 28.

Artusi, P. (1960) *La scienza in cucina e l'arte di mangiar bene: Manuale pratico per le famiglie.* [*Science in the kitchen and the art of eating well: a practical guide for families*, Italian] (1st ed. Florence: self-published, 1891) Florence: Giunti Marzocco.

Baker, J. *San Martino* by Giosuè Carducci. English trans. featured on *John Baker's blog: Reflections of a working writer and reader*, [online] 19 March 2008. Available at http://johnbakersblog.co.uk/giosue-carducci/; accessed November 2011.

Barzini, L. (1991) *The Italians*. London: Penguin Books.

Capatti, A. & Montanari, M. (2003) *Italian cuisine: A cultural history.* [*La cucina Italiana: Storia di una cultura*, English] Trans. A. O'Healy. New York: Columbia University Press.

Dickie, J. (2007) *Delizia! The epic history of the Italians and their food.* London: Hodder & Stoughton. US edition, 2008; New York: Free Press.

Godek, G. J. P. (1999) *10,000 ways to say I love you*. Naperville, Illinois: Sourcebooks, Inc.

LaLudesana (2009) Tipico Lodigiano cheese. [Online] Available at http://www.laludesana.com/products.php; accessed November 2011.

Mortadella Bologna (2007) The taste of the best tradition [*Il sapore della migliore tradizione*, English] [online]. Available at www.mortadellabologna.com; accessed February 2012.

Regione Lombardia, Directorate-General Agriculture & Unioncamere Lombardia (2011) 'Nourishing Culture' programme and 'Food Education project', both part of the Buonalombardia initiative, [online]. Available at www.buonalombardia.it; accessed November 2011.

Severgnini, B. (2007) *La bella figura: A field guide to the Italian mind.* Hodder & Stoughton. [*Testa degli Italiani*, English] Trans. G. Watson. p. 26.

Verri, P. (1783) *Storia di Milano*. Milan: Stamperia di Guiseppe Marelli.

Wright, C. A. (2007) Risotto alla Milanese. [Online] Available at www.cliffordawright.com; accessed November 2011.

Index